UP FROM THE ASHES

Jackie Goddard

Published by:
Ripple Effect Publishing,
The Poetry Shop, Moniaive,
Dumfriesshire. DG3 4HN
Telephone: 01848 200322

© Jackie Goddard 2001

All rights reserved. No part of this publication may be reproduced in any form, except for the purposes of review, without prior written permission from the copyright owner.

British Library Cataloguing in Publication Data. A catalogue record for this book is available from the British Library.

ISBN 0-9540796-0-4

I would like to take this opportunity to acknowledge the use of other people's words in this book.

Artwork by Twenty 3 Crows Ltd, Moniaive
Printed by MFP Design & Print, Manchester.
Front cover illustration by Jade Goddard.

THIS BOOK IS

DEDICATED TO

TWO SPECIAL LADIES

CALLED ELIZABETH

ACKNOWLEDGEMENTS

My love and grateful thanks go to so many people that I hardly know where to begin.

To my wonderful husband Dean and my three fantastic children, Jade Lee and Rory – thank you for all you've been through for me and with me. You know I couldn't have done it without you.
To my dad, for all your strength and support, and for the courage I got from you to write this.
To my mum, if only you were here with me today.
To my brother and sister, just for being themselves.
To Eileen, Lynn and Marion, thank you for your love, hugs and prayers.
To Christine, for your faith, support and understanding.
To all of my friends who have been with me from the start and helped me through.
To Janice, thanks for making me laugh so much and being a shoulder to cry on at times.
To Liz, thank you for your obvious enjoyment of my story and for your company on so many days, the good ones and the bad.
To Peter, for all your help with cutting and pasting, and then proof reading till we were almost word blind.
To Ian and Christine, for their help and support.
To Sue, for your great skills, your fresh eye and for tying up the loose ends.
To Hugh, for all your mad travel stories and mountains of cakes and biscuits.
To Paul and Sharon, for your help, advice, and endless patience, and for letting me borrow your broom!

My very special thanks also go to:
My friend Senga, for supplying me with copious amounts of alcohol and the use of her pool table and jukebox – and the rest!

To Lesley, for believing in the ripple effect and her patience on those nights when we've all partied on way past her bedtime!

To my 'happy daftie' neighbour Debbie, thanks for all the wine and mushrooms that I promise to return one day!

To lovely Auntie Pearl, Dean's only other 'partner'!

To Uncle Jack, for coming in to light your pipe almost every day!

Thanks to Rick, hopefully he will now have to admit that I've got more than space between my ears!

To all the regulars at 'The Sunday Club'.

To all my pals, young and old, who have come into the shop on a regular basis over the past two years, thanks for your company – even though you may have often feared for your safety in here!

To John Carter, for your up front and honest opinion.

My thanks to everyone in the media who has been intrigued enough to write an article about me, especially Margaret Clayton, who wrote the first one.

To all my customers, for your appreciation of my work, your kind cards, letters and comments.

To anyone else who has given me any help, advice and encouragement – many thanks.

And finally -

To anyone who has ever gossiped about me - have a nice life, because mine is pretty fantastic now - and I wish you all that you deserve in yours!

UP FROM
THE ASHES

Chapter 1

I'm going to tell my story now and, although it starts in a fairly serious vein, I can guarantee that it will make a lot of people smile, laugh and even cry in places. You may also be intrigued now and then because that word has figured many times in conversations I've had over the past two years.

At this moment I'm not famous so many people won't have a clue who I am but, by the time you've read my story, you will know me very well indeed and I think you will probably quite like me and my wonderful batty family.

Having said I'm not famous I should now point out that I have begun to become more widely known because of a very unique and unusual new venture that I happened upon purely by chance. By rights my business should be called Serendipity because of this, but the name I have chosen has a great deal more significance to me for reasons that will eventually become clear as you read the story.

My company name is Ripple Effect Publishing. It's a very familiar term, easy to understand and I'm delighted to say that since it started I've been causing quite a few ripples which have produced a great deal of fun and hilarity since I came out of my shell in September 98.

So what is this new, unique and unusual venture? It's very simple – I write humorous poetry!

For those of you who are now thinking "big deal" and beginning to wonder if it's worth reading any further I can assure you that it really is a very big deal to me. And as you will soon realise I am having some of the best times of my life now that I have discovered what to do with my work.

I've been writing poems for over ten years now, mainly in a humorous vein and based on the life of a mum and very grudging housewife. After a stressful, harassed day I would write a silly poem about it to get it out of my system. For years these poems sat gathering dust in my desk drawer, still in hand written form, but friends and family kept telling me I should do something with them. I didn't know what to do with them then – but by God I do now!

In November 1998 I finally plucked up the courage and decided to see what the public thought so I rented a stall for a few weeks in our local shopping centre. I had all of my poems printed in black and white A4 format and sold them at £1 each as unusual Christmas stocking fillers and the response I got was quite overwhelming. Even though I had expected them to appeal mainly to women I was highly amused to note that a lot of my customers were husbands and children who obviously recognised their own wives and mums in the poems.

At the same time I was asked so often whether I sold the complete set that I decided to make them up into a very basic booklet form to use up my stock. I'm happy to say that not only did they sell very well on the stall but I have since sold a great many in the shop as well as through mail order and my stock is diminishing rapidly. Eventually I may have them printed in a more professional format and that book will contain many more poems I have written since then.

These booklets keep being referred to as an anthology by people who are more familiar with publishing and poetry terminology. I personally don't take my work seriously enough to give it such a pompous title but I suppose I have to admit that this is the word that describes it best. Therefore the title of my first anthology is called 'My Life In Rhyme' and that's exactly what it is. There are poems on many different subjects - about being 40, housework, children, pets, being hard up, being overweight etc. It also includes a few on more serious subjects such as the environment and the mess we are making of our world and a poem written as a tribute for Armistice Day which I have used to raise funds for The Lady Haig Poppy Appeal.

As well as writing and selling my own work I discovered a market for personalised poetry, something I had never even considered and was not aware I could do but was asked for so many times that I decided to have a go. The response has been absolutely incredible and to date I have written in the region of 300 personalised poems! They have covered almost every occasion you care to mention from birthdays, weddings, best man and father of the bride speeches, new born, leaving, get well and even, sadly, several bereavement poems.

I now have a file full of hundreds of wonderful thank you cards and letters from customers the length and breadth of Britain as well as at least ten other countries ranging from Canada, America and Australia to Bermuda and even Vietnam.

So after my time was up on the stall I came home full of enthusiasm and absolutely determined that I was no longer going to be stuck at home as a housewife – apart from anything else I never liked that job anyway! I would like to stress that although I love being a mum I have never enjoyed the boring routine of 'keeping house' but I used to think it was all I could do to contribute to the dire situation we were in financially.

Since the failure of a business venture in the mid 1980's we had been in serious debt for many years. As a result of this we were not in a position to have a fancy home with all 'mod cons' so we made do with second hand carpets and mismatched furniture, mostly passed on to us. Our 'house' was not perfect in that sense but I kept it as clean and tidy as I could for all those years and it was always thought of by our friends and family as a lovely, welcoming 'home'. Given the choice even today I would still rather have a cosy muddle of a home than a perfect, sterile palace.

My husband Dean worked very, very hard throughout this period struggling to pay off our debts while I stayed at home with the children, making sure I was there when they came home from school. In those days I used to do a lot of home baking so that there was always something warm and substantial for them to eat. They tell me now they have wonderful memories of wandering down the lane and being able to smell my soups and home made stews long before they reached the house.

This then was my contribution and, although I confess to being a grudging housewife, I am still very proud of those years and the memories they contain for my children.

When we had decided to start a family I vowed that I would always be there for them and not go out to work while they were young. I hasten to add that I am not trying to cast any aspersions on mums who do, it was just something I was determined not to do. Added to this, even if I had been inclined to do so, I would probably only have been suited to a fairly low paid job because I had no real qualifications and was completely baffled by the computer age. This would have meant that most of my wages would have gone on childcare so it was not worth the disruption to our family.

In 1993 another event occurred that very definitely decided us that I would not be going out to work because at the age of 37 I discovered I was pregnant again! By the time Rory was born in October of that year our daughter Jade was almost eleven and our son Lee was eight. At this point I should bring in the word Serendipity again because I was seriously tempted to make that Rory's middle name!

My own interpretation of the word is that it means 'happening upon something wonderful purely by chance' which is not exactly the dictionary definition but it's close enough for me.

So with this fantastic new addition to our family we continued to struggle on for more years. Most people who have been in financial trouble themselves will be familiar with the term 'robbing Peter to pay Paul' and that was all we could do.

There was never enough money to pay every bill each month so we tried to space them out evenly, paying one bill one month and missing that to pay another the next. We borrowed money to try and consolidate our debts and get things under control but then something unexpected would come along and all our plans and budgets went out the window. Then we borrowed more to get out of that mess and so it went on.

During all of this time I became more and more withdrawn

and kept myself hidden away in our rotten, damp, leaky, rented farmhouse because I was embarrassed and ashamed. I knew we were being gossiped about but felt powerless to stop it so I made very few friends and was rarely seen in the village. We had a small circle of good, trusted friends who were aware of our problems and how they came about and our families were always there to give us as much support and help as they could.

Many times during those years we felt as though we were drowning in debt and the stress on both of us was almost unbearable. A lot of marriages would have crumbled under the weight of it all – it only made ours stronger.

There were occasions when Dean would come home from a hard days work to find me weeping because there had been another threatening letter about our debts or a stroppy phone call – some days I wouldn't even have the courage to answer the phone. He would comfort me, more often than not send me to bed to rest, then he would just roll up his sleeves and get on with cooking the dinner, doing some housework and looking after the children.

Again a lot of people will know the paralysing effect this sort of stress can have, not to mention the feelings of humiliation when you try to apply for any benefits you think you may be entitled to and you very often have to endure being spoken to in a patronising, rude or offhand manner. This attitude often left me feeling that these people thought because we were unable to control our debts we must obviously be of low intelligence or that we deserved what we'd got.

In those days I often used to think I was heading for a nervous breakdown. I felt that I'd lost the ability to laugh and became more and more paranoid about gossip. I realised we were not the only ones being talked about of course, but I hated the fact that we were under discussion at all and that we had no control over it. People who had no idea of who we were and what we were going through were casually discussing us in the local shops, Post Office and pubs and there was nothing we could do to stop it.

One of the many reasons I'm enjoying myself so much these days is that I know who most of these people are! I have also learned things about some of them that would make your toes curl but that I will never use against them because I detest gossip with a vengeance. I've even written a poem about the subject that has been read by hundreds of people or that I have read out to them and their reactions have been fantastic. I thought it might be a good idea to intersperse a lot of my poems throughout the book at the appropriate times and I think this is a good one to start the ball rolling so here it is.

HAVE YOU HEARD THE LATEST?

I think gossip is like Chinese Whispers
Where you start with an innocent word
By the time it gets round to the last one
    The story's become quite absurd.

If you're playing the game at a party
You can say what you like, just for fun
It's a game, so the truth doesn't matter
And you have a good laugh – no harm done.

In reality though, it's quite different
It's important to get the facts right
We all know how gossip gets twisted
    Just to give it a little more bite.

So one day someone tells you a story
That they've heard – but it's not from the source
And they've added their own little version
But that's just their opinion of course!

> Then the story goes on to the next one
> With a word or two changed, but who cares
> And soon it's beyond recognition
> The original facts are not there.
>
> Do you ever consider the damage
> And the hurt and the pain that is caused
> When you talk for your own entertainment
> Don't you think the next time you should pause?
>
> Just imagine how you'd feel in their shoes
> It's a sad fact of life, but it's true
> That it might just be your turn tomorrow
> And the gossip will be about you.
>
> So remember that famous old saying
> Try to 'do unto others' from now
> And the next time that someone spreads poison
> Tell them just where to stick it – and how!

So you can probably tell just how strong my feelings are and I have been sorely tempted to post that particular poem through a few letterboxes I can tell you!

Taking my own advice, I now have this knowledge about a lot of people that is like a secret weapon and, though I will never use it, it is such a comfort to have. Instead I look these people straight in the eye nowadays and am so sickeningly polite to them I can almost see them squirm. I even have it in my heart to feel sorry for them because they obviously have such empty, sad and frustrated lives that I feel they are more to be pitied than scolded (as my beloved mum used to say).

Having digressed a bit, as I will no doubt do many times throughout the story, I should now return to the point where I knew I had to continue with my work and no longer wanted to hide away. I felt strong enough to face people and wanted to work in the public eye so I rented a shop in the village that had lain empty for years, tidied it up over a period of time and filled it with comfy old sofas and chairs. In April of 1999 I quietly opened the door and waited to see what would happen.

I was well aware that when the sign went up above my door that said this was 'The Poetry Shop' that a lot of people would be saying "what the hell is she doing – she must have lost her marbles" or words to that effect. What most of them didn't realise at the time was that I never expected any custom from locals. Most of my business came by mail or phone orders and I already had a very strong customer base from my time on the stall and that was growing daily.

What I intended for the local people was for the shop to be a drop-in centre where they could come for a cuppa and a chat whilst waiting for buses or children to come out of school or just somewhere to meet up with friends. There are a number of board games and jigsaws and a selection of toys for youngsters of all ages as well as several shelves of second hand books. There's no charge for any of it but there is a donations box which people have been happy to contribute to and the proceeds help replenish stocks of tea and coffee etc and have also been used to help the primary school with some money towards their Christmas party – just one small example of the ripple effect!

Over the next couple of months people gradually began to call in on a regular basis and a lot of tourists and visitors were intrigued enough to come in, often staying for much longer than intended and usually leaving with a copy of my anthology.

By July I felt very positive about the interest shown and decided it was time to have an official 'Grand Opening' for the shop so I sent invitations out to customers, family and friends. To coincide with the day there was a wonderful article written about it in The Sunday Post by a lady called Margaret Clayton and the response to that was unbelievable. For several weeks after I was inundated with phone calls and letters, not only ordering poems but from a lot of people congratulating me on the idea itself. Several of these were women who had written personalised poems themselves for friends and family and they said that I could call on them for help if I became too busy.

I have already used one of these women on several occasions and have another half dozen names which I've kept on file because I know there will come a time, in the not too distant future, when I'll have to step back from the personalised side of things in order to concentrate on my other work. It would be nice to think these women could be employed to work in the comfort of their own homes, doing work they thoroughly enjoy and getting a decent wage for it instead of the insulting amounts offered by some of these 'home working schemes' where you have to put in a lot of hours and end up being paid peanuts. I suppose you could say that's another example of the ripple effect!

Chapter 2

In the months that followed I continued to enjoy myself, got to know some wonderful people and my confidence grew daily. I knew I had stumbled upon something very unique that at the same time was giving me the opportunity to lay a lot of ghosts. It also enabled me to 'get my own back' on a number of people who had been both rude and insulting about my venture.

An example of this was in November 1998 while I was still on the stall. It was very early in the month and because Armistice Day was approaching I had felt moved to write a tribute poem to commemorate the occasion. I was actually sitting not three feet away from my dad, an ex-soldier, when I wrote it and it was quite an emotional time I have to say.

After it was written it occurred to me that it would be a good way of raising funds for a very worthy cause so I offered it for sale with 50% of the proceeds going to The Lady Haig Poppy Fund. A minister from Lockerbie asked permission to use it in his Remembrance Day service and my own minister used it as well and sold 48 copies in one morning.

At the same time I thought that it might be an idea to offer it to one of our local newspapers to include in an article they were doing for Armistice that week so that it would become more widely known and therefore help to raise even more funds.

However, as a result of my phone call to the editor (who shall remain nameless!) I was accused of 'jumping on the charity bandwagon'!

It appeared he was more concerned about the other 50% and didn't seem to appreciate that not only was I picking up all the printing and packaging costs etc but that I'd had no need to offer any of it for fundraising and could have kept it all.

I'm happy to say that his attitude did not put me off and I am still using the poem to raise funds. I also had occasion to stand right beside the man in question some months later and had the pleasure of blanking him completely. Childish maybe, but very satisfying all the same. This is the poem that he refused to print.

A TRIBUTE – LEST WE FORGET

In Flanders there is a field full of poppies
And they represent suffering and pain
Young men gave their lives for their country
And their families never saw them again.

Now each year at this time we buy poppies
To remember those soldiers who died
Did they know, when they left all their loved ones
That they would leave them a legacy of pride?

It was pride for their sons and their brothers
Their fathers, their uncles, their kin
And if we cannot stop causing bloodshed
Does this mean that they all died in vain?

Look around at who's wearing those poppies
See the ages of them, young and old
Do not think for a moment we care not
We have asked and your story's been told.

We are wearing our poppies in tribute
For your courage and the blood that you spilled
But for you we would have no tomorrow
For our lives this day, you were killed.

For my dad, for his friends, for all soldiers
There are no words to express how we feel
You gave us your lives and we thank you
We did not forget – never will.

Another example on the negative side was from someone who did not take a pop at me personally but at the whole village!

We live in a beautiful little village in South West Scotland called Moniaive (pronounced Mon-ee-ive) and a reporter from a very well known newspaper came here for two weeks in 1999, ostensibly to write a book. At the same time, however, she wrote a very insulting and negative article about our village and I was incensed when I read it. A great number of other people were also annoyed because not only were some of her facts wrong but it had been written in such a fashion as to make Moniaive seem very dull and boring with nothing to attract tourists.

This small community is teeming with talent - we have dozens of writers, artists and musicians as well as a lot of fascinating history, great hotels and some fabulous characters, one of whom I have to confess is my own dear old dad who I have also written a poem about.

The newspaper printed one excellent and very sarcastic response from a resident but I felt the editor should be made aware of just how many more of us had been really angered by the article. A lot of people wrote individual letters and comments and I, you might be surprised to hear, wrote her a poem. It was an invitation to come back and see us again and give us a chance to tell her exactly what we thought of her article.

Needless to say she did not accept but instead sent me a short, sarcastic note saying that if she ever returned to the area she would be staying with 'intimate friends' and would be keeping as low a profile as possible. You can just imagine some of the comments that were made when that was shown around!

She also went on to say that she had looked into the window of my shop but that 'alas, she had not felt compelled to come in' and I have to say I am eternally grateful that she did not. It's also interesting to note that she left the village the day before the article was published!

Before I print the poem I sent her I should explain that one of the biggest mistakes she made was a reference to one of the hotels in the village. We have two hotels in the main street, one of which is famous for having a 'tramps hole' – a small space above the fireplace where people used to put money and any passing tramp could use it to buy himself a meal or a drink. Since there are only two hotels to choose from you'd think she might have got the right one but in fact she reported this as being in the other hotel. Another part of the article scathingly suggested that the people of the village did nothing but sit around drinking coffee and eating biscuits all day. I've mentioned these two points because I've referred to them in the poem so now the verses should make more sense.

COME INTO MY PARLOUR!

Correct me if I'm wrong here
But I always understood
That to be a news reporter
Then your research must be good.

To write a decent article
Your facts should be correct
And if you are at all unsure
Then you check and double check

But I chanced upon a story
Where the 'author' claimed she'd been
In person, to our village
And she wrote of what she'd seen

But the more I read, I have to say
The less I believed my eyes
I don't know where she thought she was
But it wasn't Moniaive!

So I asked in The Craigdarroch
That's the one without the hole
I asked as well in The George Hotel
And guess what I was told?

It seems I'm not the only one
To be incensed by all her blurb
You've printed one reply so far
There's more to come, I've heard

But would she have the nerve, I ask
To visit us again
I have the perfect venue
Though it has the strangest name

I'm sure it would be just the place
Even though it may sound absurd
I doubt if she's heard of The Poetry Shop
But it's the only one in the world!

So now you have our gauntlet
Pop along and get the facts
And of course you'll get a coffee
Even a biscuit come to that

May I suggest as well, Ms Khan
That you bring a dictaphone
Then the margin for your errors
Should be a much, much slimmer one!

So there! I suppose it's hardly surprising she didn't accept the invitation considering she obviously didn't even have the nerve to stay around in the first place! Although I've had to shelve this matter for some time I am still determined to redress the balance one day – perhaps by getting a much more favourable piece written at some time in the future by another more discerning and responsible reporter. Who knows, the day may also come when I actually come face to face with our old friend – rest assured, I will savour the moment!

The only other really negative thing to occur within my first year in the shop was unexpected but it has since caused myself and many other people so much amusement that I am actually quite glad that it did happen.

Just a few days after Christmas 1999 I came into the shop to check for mail and messages and found an anonymous letter had been hand delivered through my door. I remember being quite shocked at its contents for about half an hour and then feeling very angry. Dean was with me at the time and although it goes completely against his nature if he could have lain hands on the authors at that moment he would have punched their lights out!

However, what we did instead was to stroll down to the pub and have a think about it. The content of the letter was basically telling me that the 'authors' thought I wrote "crap, clean lyrics with no style or content discernible" and they were apparently annoyed that I could make a living out of it.

They also seemed to think that I was being funded by some other outside source and felt the money should go to far more deserving causes. They went on to dare me (with a few choice expletives included) to put a response in my window. Once my anger had abated I began to see the funny side of it so, instead of wasting my valuable time writing back to them, I had the letter photocopied. I blanked out the offensive words, and displayed it in my shop window for a few weeks with a note saying that "apparently not everyone approved of my new venture".

I should also tell you that I discovered their identities in less than a week via a mutual acquaintance – one of the more positive sides to a small community grapevine!

Obviously I can't print the original letter because it's too offensive but over the next few weeks I took great pleasure in passing my 'fan mail' round as publicly as possible, taking pains to let everyone know how amused I was and knowing that word would eventually get back to them.

The only thing that troubled me was that the authors were connected to families in the village with whom I had no quarrel and I felt they would be annoyed and embarrassed if they knew about it. Stranger still was the fact that at least one person involved rarely comes to the village and I would not have known them if I'd fallen over them in the street!

So I thought no more of it for quite a time although every now and then a line or two of response would come to me and I would scribble it down.

Then in June 2000, whilst having a grand clean up in the shop, I came across several sheets of 'one liners' and realised the finished article was there, it just needed to be rearranged.

I typed it up into a five verse 'response' called 'To My Anonymous Fans' and I have since read it out to dozens of people who read the original. It has received rounds of applause, roars of laughter and even an encore or two. I've also let it be known that if the authors would like to come along with £20 each they can collect their order anytime!

A famous phrase by a man called Thomas Bulwer Lytton has occurred to me many times since this venture began and that is that 'the pen is mightier than the sword'. I now realise I am being given the chance to wield my pen mightily and I am loving every minute of it. My confidence has grown to such an extent that I feel I can cope with anyone, no matter how rude or insulting they are about what I do.

I never expected it to appeal to everyone but the fact remains that I have entertained and amused thousands of people in just the two years I've been in business so the opinions of the small minority of people in comparison who don't like my work don't concern me at all.

What I also now realise is that we as a family are good, decent people who mean no harm to anyone and we intend to continue that way, despite the fact we are still being gossiped about from several quarters. It doesn't trouble me at all nowadays but I know that Dean still gets angry about it on occasion because we are aware that some of it is coming from church going people who would like to be thought of as good Christians but who are in fact the worst type of hypocrites.

What always used to baffle me, and still does, is why do they do it? Most of these people know nothing about us and have never taken the trouble to find out – probably because the true story would be nowhere near as entertaining as listening to someone else's version. The fact is there really isn't much to tell. The one and only 'crime' we ever committed was to get into serious debt and struggle with it for many years. That's it – that's all there is to it!

I'm delighted to say that Dean's work has gone from strength to strength over the years so our financial situation is getting easier and I am so pleased for him and so proud. He deserves nothing less after the hard, hard slog he's had where I was sometimes so scared he would be crushed under the weight of it. He would drive off some mornings looking so tense and worried that I was terrified. My imagination would run riot and I would picture him driving but not really concentrating because he had so much on his mind and then having an accident. Thankfully God has been looking out for him all this time and it never happened.

As for me I'm making loads of great new friends and having the time of my life in my shop – so much so that it's a pleasure to come to work every day. Although we still have a fair way to go before we can consider ourselves solvent things are definitely improving, albeit slowly, and we can see an end in sight.

Our close friends and family who stood by us are now so

happy for us, they always knew the whole story and believe that we really deserve our change of fortune. Of course if my venture continues to take off and I become more widely known there is even a chance that I could start making a profit and be able to contribute as well! The truth is that if I had been doing this work from home for the past two years I could have a tidy sum in the bank by now but at the moment it all goes towards the overheads on the shop.

However, I feel very positive that in time to come I will start making 'proper' money and now that I've been here so long and am used to having so many people call in every day I couldn't bear to go back to working from home. I have to admit that our house has never been the same since I started this but I don't really care!

We finally moved out of the grotty farmhouse in November 1999 into our first owned home in the village but it is so much smaller and with five of us, a cat and two Great Danes you can appreciate that it is almost always in a state of absolute chaos. We do try, between us all (even little Rory insists on helping by drying dishes and hoovering) but no matter how much we do it seems to take just a matter of hours for it to be reduced to a shambles again. I've come to the conclusion that the minute our back is turned the dishes and laundry start to breed like rabbits but do I care? Not in the slightest! I know that we will eventually get ourselves sorted out and return to some semblance of normality but we are so used to muddling through that it really doesn't trouble us very often. There are still days when it causes tension and we can all get a bit uptight but more often than not we just laugh our way out of it.

This next poem was inspired by a conversation with another mum last year while we were both having a moan about the drudgery of housework. It was printed in The Sunday Post article I mentioned earlier, and was so well received that I sold dozens of individual copies of it.

AM I ALONE?

The thing about housework that bugs me
Is that I don't want to do it at all
You're meant to keep things nice and tidy
'Cos you never know when folk might call.

So each day you must go though the motions
You hoover and dust and make beds
Pick up toys, clean the loo and do laundry
Then of course they've all got to be fed.

But I don't give a damn, to be truthful
I think housework's a right royal pain
And the worst of it all is each morning
You have to start over again!

Well I don't lose much sleep if it's dusty
If there are crumbs on the carpet – who cares?
The ironing gets done as it's needed
And everyone does their own share.

'Cos in our house we all pitch together
It's not 'my' work, it's 'ours', which is fair
But if the kitchen's reduced to a shambles
When they cook, then the dishes are theirs!

So although it's not spotless, it's 'lived in'
It's a home, not a house on display
And the world won't stop turning I'm certain
If I don't 'hoover through' every day!

You've no doubt guessed that housework is something I hate almost as much as gossip but it's not to say that I wouldn't love to have a nice tidy home and we will get there in the end I know.

We intend to make a start on seriously renovating and decorating the house fairly soon but at the moment it's a question of finding the time as much as the money. Needless to say when we do start I'll be the first one into the kitchen with a crow bar!

As I said though, we usually manage to laugh our way out of tense situations these days and that is probably the single most important factor about my work to me - that it has helped me to find my sense of humour again and has entertained a lot of other people in the process. It's also given me the courage to face people and know that we have nothing to hide any more – I look people square in the eye these days and if they can't meet my gaze then that's their problem. I sometimes find it hard to believe that it's only been a couple of years since I came out of my shell but I am so brave now, so 'in your face' that I'm not afraid of anyone any more, and I never will be again.

Chapter 3

My work is continuing to grow at a rapid pace now and since the original Sunday Post article I've had at least another dozen written about the shop in various newspapers and magazines. I have also appeared on local television and Radio Scotland and each time this generates more interest and orders. Some of my customers for personalised poems have come back for second, third and even fourth orders and the letters and cards they send after the event are so touching that I'm often moved to tears.

A lot of them tell me that the recipients were very emotional and cried but more often than not the poems have produced laughter, especially the best man and father of the bride speeches. They are always so appreciated because they say making a speech is a nerve-racking experience anyway so to be able to make the audience laugh almost immediately helps the speaker to relax as well.

The hardest ones to write are obviously bereavement poems because they are so heart rending. I get very emotional myself when I write them but I feel it's a privilege to be asked to help people in their time of grief.

Apart from the personalised side I'm continuing to write my own mainly humorous poems which as I said before may eventually be turned into a much larger anthology – truth to tell it's likely to be an enormous volume because I could write a poem every day about some of the mad things that happen in our family and in the shop!

In 'My Life In Rhyme' there are two poems on the subject of Being 40, one is the up side and the other is the down side, both of which proved very popular on the stall whilst selling individually. The 'up' side is more positive and encouraging but the 'down' side is my favourite because I think it's funnier. They were written, not surprisingly, as I was approaching that particular birthday but I have to say I'm not one of these women who is concerned about getting older, quite the opposite. I believe that it's a state of mind and that it's up to you how old you want to feel – so much so that I find myself deliberately behaving badly sometimes just for the hell of it! This is probably an obvious place to introduce those two poems.

BEING 40 (The Down Side)

It's a bitch and half, being forty
It's the end of the line, some might say
Your husband starts calling you porky
And your once auburn hair has turned grey.

There are wrinkles that used to be laugh lines
From the stresses and strains of the years
And on checking the mirror at bathtime
It's enough to reduce you to tears!

'Cos your waistline has thickened by inches
And your boobs are beginning to sag
Then you zip up your skirt and it pinches
And your skin's like an old leather bag!

And your memory's a bit of a let down
You have trouble recalling a name
And you've not even had thirty seconds
Never mind fifteen minutes of fame!

I'm not sure and I might just be guessing
But I feel that there's life in me still
I don't want to be old and depressing
I don't want to be over the hill!

That's the negative viewpoint, now here comes the other one!

BEING 40 (The Up Side)

When you're twenty you're full of ambition
When you're thirty there's still time to shine
But why is it when you hit forty
It's considered the end of the line?

Well, I'm forty and nowhere near finished
In fact I have hardly begun
There are dozens of dreams to accomplish
Many things that I still haven't done.

I want to take German at night school
There's a lady who'll teach me to jive
I'll be camping in France next September
And I still have to learn how to drive.

I must take a course on computing
'Cos my children all think it's a scream
That I can finish the Telegraph crossword
But can't even start their machine!

And then there's my best selling novel
Which is written up here in my head
I must get it all down on paper
Or how will it ever get read?

And I still have to make some enquiries
About starting an art class next year
Or I might have a go at aerobics
'Cos I've already got all the gear.

So it's not such a bitch, being forty
It's when life begins, so to speak
How dare they suggest that I'm over the hill
When I'm only just reaching my peak!

I confess I haven't done all that well with that list of ambitions but I have achieved the most important one because I am getting it all down on paper and it is being read!

As for the others I won't be taking any art classes or jiving lessons, I've given up on learning to drive and I hate exercise but I would still like to learn German and go camping in France.

I have also reluctantly learned a bit about computers because I realise the need for it in my work but I am such a technophobe that I had to be dragged along kicking and screaming! I really don't like the way computers are becoming so insidious in our lives, especially now that the Internet is such a big thing. I think of them as a necessary evil so I refuse to learn any more about them than I have to.

I have a web site which is now really out of date and I can't be bothered to do anything about it and I have an email address that I never check because I don't know how to although every so often Dean or Jade will do it for me. Jade even wrote me out idiot-proof instructions so that I could do it myself but I lost them! The truth is I would rather receive a letter in the mail or hear a voice on the other end of the phone, it's much more personal.

While we're on the subject of technology I also have a mobile phone I rarely use, Jade had to write me instructions for that as well because it took me ages to remember which button to press to answer it and half the time it rings I don't even realise it's mine so the caller's hung up before it dawns on me.

So there you have it, when it comes to the techno age I'm as thick as mince and proud of it!

Chapter 4

Although I am becoming recognised for the poetry side of my work I really did happen upon it by accident. Before that I wrote a number of different things, one of which was a short children's book for Jade and Lee, long before Rory was born. It was very rough around the edges but not bad for a first attempt I think and I intend to dust it off one day, tidy it up and get it published.

As well as that I'm part way through a humorous novel, not too loosely based on my own dear, batty family where two of the central characters are my dad and our oldest, cowardly and very flatulent Great Dane!

I was still working on that when I first opened the shop and had written somewhere in the region of 30,000 words but it had to be shelved when I started to get busy and I've never looked at it since. However, I think once this first volume is complete I will go back to the novel for a while because I know it would take very little time to get it finished.

Apart from the orders all of my publicity have generated I've also been amazed at the number of people who have called to thank me for inspiring them! A lot of them have been writing both prose and poetry for years but only thought of it as a hobby and now they've decided to take it further. I've even had people writing to me or calling in to the shop who've composed a poem about me!

One other fascinating point that has emerged whilst talking to other writers is about self-confidence, or sometimes the lack of it. I used to think it was so weird that I could have 'good days and bad days' and often thought I was on the way to losing my marbles!

I can come into the shop some mornings absolutely brimming with confidence and ideas and feeling I could convince anyone that what I do is worth a mention. On days like that I can pick up the phone or write a letter to a variety of people in the media, telling them what I'm doing in such an enthusiastic way that very often I get their attention and an article follows.

On other days however, and for no apparent reason, I feel very nervous and unsure of myself and I wonder if I'm ever going to get anywhere. Fortunately the good days far outweigh the bad ones and it doesn't usually take me long to shake myself out of the mood. It helps too that I only have to look at the walls that are plastered with previous write-ups and all the fantastic letters and cards I've had and I know that my work has been appreciated so that acts as a boost as well.

Added to that I've had several nice, encouraging letters from well known people such as Doctor Hilary Jones, Lorraine Kelly and Dudley Russell (husband and manager of Pam Ayres) that I've kept on file and I've had one or two tentative enquiries from afternoon TV chat shows asking me if I would be prepared to go on and talk about my work.

As yet nothing has been finalised because they seem to think they need a poetry theme on their programmes so that they could fit me in but eventually I might be able to convince them otherwise!

The truth is I'd like to have the chance to tell my story to a much larger audience because I've been told by so many people that it's an inspiring one. At this point I should tell you that I started this autobiography last year and wrote the first twenty pages in the space of just a few days which I then copied several times and started passing round to see what would happen. I apologise for using this phrase yet again but the response was overwhelming.

Within a few weeks it had been read by over four hundred people - friends, family and even complete strangers and the result was that a lot of them came back, not only to return the book but also to bring all sorts of donations for the shop.

These donations ranged from books, games and toys for the youngsters to such things as a kettle, a toaster, a fridge, a mini cooker, a microwave and even a dishwasher!

It seems that reading just those first few pages helped them to realise exactly what I'm doing and why and the most repeated comments I've had is that a lot of them could identify with it and they thought the story was inspirational.

There were also times when some of them wanted to share a little bit of their own story because they recognised a lot of similarities in their lives and mine and no longer felt there was anything to be embarrassed about.

Like I said before I now know that we have nothing to be ashamed of, writing this has been incredibly therapeutic and to know that it has helped others is a fantastic bonus. I intend to continue with the story and to be absolutely up front and honest but at the same time I intend it to be very funny in parts because there has been a lot more laughter than tears in my life.

I also know that a lot of people won't approve but frankly I don't give a damn!

Chapter 5

OK – I think it's time to return to the subject of this village and explain a bit more about it and some of the people here. Although I have already vented my spleen about the gossips I would like to stress that they are in a tiny minority and that the rest of them are mainly good, kind, friendly and decent people who, although some are still baffled about what I am doing, in the main wish me well.

In the time I've been in the shop I've made so many friends and got to know so many people of all ages that I'm quite staggered when I think of it. They range in age from toddlers, who come in with their parents and play with an odd assortment of toys while their mums and dads have a cuppa, to some of the oldest residents.

There are also a number of youngsters aged between twelve and twenty who come in on a regular basis and who I think are now beginning to see me as an eccentric 'auntie' figure – batty but harmless!

They come in and talk to each other while I work away in the background or they come in and talk to me on their own, sometimes with a problem they want some advice about and other times just because they're bored and want some company. Either way they are always welcome and I'm chuffed that they feel comfortable here.

I love the odd mixture of ages I sometimes get in all at once as well. There have been times when it has ranged from twelve to eighty and they all sit comfortably talking together whereas before these same people may have done nothing more than nod and smile to each other for years.

One other regular visitor is our lady minister Christine who is also a friend of the family. She has been in on what I'm trying to do right from the start and she calls in every so often to check on how things are going.

She knows there is a lot more to the shop than just poetry and is aware of the events that finally led to my metamorphosis and that what I'm doing now has a far greater significance than most people are even aware of. Suffice to say the name I chose for my company has a lot to do with it and that my business 'front' is just the tip of a very large iceberg!

To get back to the people here – this village has some wonderful older characters and a lot of great youngsters. The younger ones on the whole are polite, respectful and well behaved and I think very highly of them so I'm quick to defend them if I hear anyone complaining. Granted they can be a bit loud, occasionally have silly squabbles (which are usually resolved very quickly) and some of them have even been known to get drunk now and then but it's no more than most of us did at their age, whether we care to admit it or not.

I often think that half the problem with the ones who do all the moaning is that they just can't stand to see the young ones having fun because they've forgotten how to do it themselves. As far as I'm concerned there is no generation gap – we can all build bridges.

I think this is a good place to print my next poem, which is one of my more recent ones and is not in the anthology but it pretty much sums up the way I feel about life now.

GROWING OLD DISGRACEFULLY

When you reach a certain age it's quite depressing
That people think it's wrong to misbehave
You have to follow different rules when you're an adult
And you're stuck with them until you're in your grave.

You're supposed to settle down as you get older
Set examples to your children as they grow
They learn by watching you, the experts tell us
So you really should be careful how you go.

But what if you still like to go and party
Let your hair down now and then and have some fun
Have a drink with friends and make a bit of whoopee
Reach the pub at eight and don't go home till one!

While you're there you love to listen to the jukebox
And you also like a game of pool as well
You enjoy a pint or two of good strong cider
And you know you shouldn't smoke but what the hell!

Then you like to boogie round the room to music
While you do the boring housework every day
And you turn the volume up so you can hear it
Above the hoover, as you dance the chores away!

Now I know that my behaviour isn't normal
I should act my age more often I suppose
But there isn't any rulebook I'm aware of
And I really don't intend to decompose!

So although I'm forty-four upon the outside
On the inside I'll remain at twenty-five
I might be going grey and have some wrinkles
But by God I know it's good to be alive!

And there you have it! After a decade or so of hiding myself away and seldom being seen in the village, let alone the pubs, I'm back with a vengeance, I'm having an absolute ball and I don't give a diddly what people think.

I am being seen regularly going into the pub at all hours, day and night, and no doubt the gossips will have their own opinions about that but I bet they'd be disappointed if they knew the whole story!

The truth is I do go in there a lot, sometimes I have a soda and lime, sometimes a cup of tea and sometimes, especially at nights, I even drink quite a few ciders! I have even been known to go in there and drink nothing at all although I'll grant you that doesn't happen very often! The reason for the daytime visits is that not only am I very friendly with the owner but about eight months ago I started playing pool so I go in there to practise because quite often it's too busy to get on the table at nights.

I have to confess that I've been aware on many occasions of having been spotted by one of the gossips whilst walking home and, even though I'd had no intention of going into the pub I've nipped in anyway. I've stopped for a quick chat and waited until the gossips have gone before I come out again then they never know how long I've stayed in there. Daft I know, but I enjoy the game!

The fact is I get on with all ages and I treat everyone with the same respect, old and young. I'm probably making it sound as though I'm friends with everyone but of course that's not the case – I am only human and there are people from around here that I can't stand the sight of! However, if they speak to me I'm civil to them but keep the conversation as brief as possible. On the other hand if they get stroppy, obnoxious or insulting I enjoy a verbal battle and I have to say that more often than not they're left reeling.

My strongest weapon is words and I love nothing more than to drop a few big ones into the conversation because most of them are plonkers who only speak in words of two syllables or less! It also helps that I have skin like a rhino when it comes to insults so you'd struggle hard to hurt my feelings.

I think one of the reasons I do get on with most folk is because I'm very blunt and honest by nature – a trait I inherited from my dad I have to say, and one that I'm very proud of.

I cannot stand people who are two-faced and sneaky and am irritated by anyone who is too scared to express an opinion. I used to be a bit of a wimp in days gone by but not any more.

Having said that I don't deliberately try to upset or offend people and if they are particularly sensitive I do make an effort to be a bit more subtle but only if I like them.

Chapter 6

I mentioned earlier that I'd written a poem about my dad and so I think this would be a good place to introduce my parents. The reason I wrote the poem, in November 1998, was that I was sitting in the pub (now there's a surprise!) beside my dad's friend Jim and watching my dad across the room having a rant about something with some poor soul and we were laughing about it. It was then that Jim suggested I should write one about dad so I did, and here it is.

WITH GRATEFUL THANKS

My dad is my hero, my mentor
Without him I would not exist
My mum's with the angels and resting
So precious and still sorely missed.

I'm an adult with children I worship
And a husband I truly adore
But if it weren't for one man I'd have nothing
For my life I have him to thank for.

I have siblings, a brother, a sister
And they love him as much as I do
We've had good times and bad times together
But united, we've always pulled through.

His life, in his youth, was not perfect
His story is too hard to tell
But the people who know him respect him
Though he's inclined to proclaim "go to hell!"

He's tough and he's blunt, but he's honest
"You can take me or leave me" he'll shout
You might like him or fear him but really
There's no other man like him about.

The mould he was cast in was broken
The day he was born, so they say
He's unique and that makes him more special
And I thank God for my dad every day.

There are times when we both have our 'off' days
And I think that he's hard and he's cold
Then I remember he's a grumpy old bugger
With a heart of just pure solid gold.

As a postscript I'd just like to mention
That his friend said I should honour him
I've wanted to tell him for ages
So for your words of wisdom – thanks Jim.

And that's my dad for you! He's 76 now and he's had some really tough times in his life, a lot of which we will probably never know about, but he's a survivor.

He was born in Plymouth to an Irish mother and a Welsh father, the second youngest of four children. His mother died when he was very young and his father was away at sea a lot and at one point he was put into the care of a children's home.

Although he has never gone into great detail about it he has told us that whilst there he was regularly beaten, so badly in fact that he has suffered kidney problems all of his life. At the age of ten he ran away from the home and lived on the road for about three years, being taught how to survive by other 'gentleman of the road'. At thirteen he lied about his age and joined the Merchant Navy for a while but eventually enlisted in the army, serving in The Black Watch for eighteen years.

It was while he was in the army that he met my mum and

he's always maintained that she was his saviour because he was, by nature, a loner and he also had a very fierce temper which often got him into trouble.

I recently gave him an A4 pad and told him he should try to write about his life because I think it would be a fascinating read and he has made a start he tells me but has to leave it at times when the memories get too much for him.

However, he comes into the shop almost every day, sometimes for just a few minutes and other times he'll sit for ages, depending on his mood. I can usually tell within seconds what kind of fettle he's in and if he's grumpy I just tell him to bugger off! We're so alike in temperament, although I'm slightly more subtle (well I think I am!) that quite often that's all it takes to make him laugh but occasionally he does just turn round and go then comes back later when he's in a better mood.

He's also quite deaf, a problem he's had since his army days during the war and often has trouble hearing, especially if there's a lot of background noise. That makes him short tempered at times but more often than not he has us in stitches when he mishears something. There can be half a dozen of us talking away in the shop and he's having a completely different conversation to the rest of us!

As you will have gathered from the first verse of the poem my darling mum is no longer with us. She died of cancer in July 1986 and even now, nearly fifteen years later, I still have days when I can't manage to talk about her without getting emotional.

Mum was born in Dublin to a Scottish mother and an Irish father but sadly her own mother died giving birth to her. She and her elder brother Christopher were brought over to Scotland when she was still a baby and raised by relatives in Ayr, so to all intents and purposes mum always thought of herself as Scottish.

Uncle Christopher was tragically killed at the age of sixteen while working as a bell-boy in a London hotel during The Blitz.

Even more tragic was the fact that during another raid just weeks later his body was blown out of it's grave and the family had to go through the whole painful process of burying him again.

I'm not clear on which of our relatives had a hand in mum and her brother's upbringing at first but my grandfather eventually remarried and I believe it was my mums stepmother who then took over, although I don't know how old mum was at the time.

My real grandmother's surname was Campbell but I'm fairly sure that most of the elderly relatives we used to visit in Ayr during our summer holidays as children were on our step-grandmother's side.

I do, however, distinctly remember visiting a family on one occasion whose surname was Campbell, they had three children, two boys and a girl, of similar age to us and they lived in Troon. They must have been relatives of mum's mum although no-one is quite clear where they fit in but eventually my sister and I would like to make the pieces fit. We did make a start on a visit to Dublin a year or so ago and we know that our grandfather's surname was Moran and that he came from a family who owned a hotel and bred racehorses. However, it appears he fell from grace because he was a bit of a gambler and was more or less thrown out of the family but he then went on to become a fairly well known chef.

Somewhere among our family memorabilia I remember seeing a menu with some famous signatures on it, one of which was that of a singer called Tessie O'Shea and it was our grandfather who'd cooked that meal apparently.

Unfortunately for us mum didn't talk much about her childhood, I think her stepmother was rather strict and not very maternal so their relationship was quite formal but mum did talk a lot of a friend called Evvie Monaghan that she went to school with. She often mentioned how the two of them would go cycling out to The Electric Brae – a favourite place for the youngsters then because of an optical illusion that made you feel you were pedalling like fury to go downhill but that you could freewheel up it!!

The only jobs I remember mum mentioning in her youth was a stint she did as a 'postie' where she actually drove for a few years (the only time in her life) and then she was a manageress in the NAAFI which was where she met and eventually married dad.

Apparently dad used to go into her canteen a lot, usually alone, and one day he gave mum a mouthful of cheek so she slapped him with a wet dishcloth – we're told that was the start of their long and beautiful friendship!

Our childhood was happy and carefree and even though there was never much money I seem to remember that most other families we knew were in the same boat so it didn't trouble us that much as children.

I know mum and dad struggled a lot for us and wanted things to be better, especially as mum had had quite a comfortable upbringing and would have liked the same for us. Dad just wanted mum to have more of the kind of life she'd been used to but because of the job situation in those days we moved around a lot and things were always quite tough financially.

I remember many summer days when we three children and some of our friends would gather by the river at the bottom of the field below the farm we lived on. We would all have a sandwich and a bottle of juice and one or two of us would bring an old inflated inner tube to share among us and we'd be there for hours on end.

I recall too that our summers then used to start on the first day of our holidays when the sun would come out and shine non-stop for the entire six weeks! It was so hot that the tar used to melt on the road and we all used to love being barefoot and bursting the tar bubbles.

We also had some wonderful holidays that wouldn't have cost much but have left me with some very special memories. Often we'd just pack everything into our old Dormobile and go off for a few days camping by a river somewhere but I also remember one holiday when we actually lived in an old train! It had four carriages, one of which was occupied by the lady who owned it and the other three were ours and I'm fairly sure it was near Largs.

So as far as I'm concerned I had a very happy childhood and it wasn't until I was much older that I appreciated the sadness and worry mum and dad had experienced. Although we knew there wasn't much money we felt very secure and loved - I think they did the best they could, which is all anyone can ask, and I'm very proud of how I turned out because of them.

Mum and I were always close, even though we had arguments when I was a teenager, and in her final years I know she was overjoyed at being a granny. She and dad would come down to visit as often as possible and they eventually moved to the area in 1985 when dad took early retirement.

Sadly it was too late for mum.

On January 1st 1986 mum told me that she'd found a lump in her breast two months earlier but hadn't wanted to tell us until Christmas was over. She had a mastectomy within a few weeks, made a wonderful recovery - and we all thought she was getting well again, but in the April she was diagnosed with a brain tumour.

She and dad had come to live with us when she was first unwell and stayed with us from then on so I nursed her at home with my sister's help.

Because of her nursing experience my sister was able to tell me on the last day that mum was failing fast so I sat with her all day, playing her favourite tapes and holding her hand, until just after ten that night, when she finally left us.
I know she's still watching over us, that she loves us and all her grandchildren, even those she never met, and I know she'll be thrilled about what I'm doing now.

Mum's poem was written in July 1990, I know it's very raw and I could adapt if I wanted to but I prefer to leave it as it is.

FOR MY PRECIOUS MUM

My mother died four years ago
Leaving a very big space in my life
"The pain will ease" they told me
"You'll be busy as a mother and a wife"

My husband and children are precious
And they helped me through very dark days
I found that I could still laugh and smile
And find wonder again through the haze.

As time passed, sure enough, it got better
As everyone told me it would
It hurts so much less when I think of her
No bad memories though, only good.

But still now and then on a bad day
I've been caught unaware and I've wished
I could see her again just to tell her
She's so precious and so very sorely missed.

Since opening the shop I have had two poetry reading evenings in different venues where people have requested particular poems but you will appreciate that this is one that I would never be able to read out in public.

Chapter 7

Now that I've introduced my parents I think it's time to talk a little bit about my brother and sister and our childhood.

I should explain though that because they are both very private people I won't be going into great detail and of course I'll ask their permission first, but I would like to mention them briefly.

My elder brother Michael was born in Ayr in 1953, the only one of the three of us to be born in Scotland - a fact of which he is immensely proud. Mum and dad had moved to married quarters in Berwick-Upon-Tweed by 1956 when I was born and were still there when my sister Kathleen arrived in 1958.

By the time we reached school age dad had left the army and we'd moved to a place called Washington in Co. Durham so we attended St. Joseph's Primary School there for a few years.

This was also where I believe my love of writing first began, all thanks to one young teacher who I'm fairly sure was called Miss Varley or something similar.

I distinctly remember her reading a book to us called Emile and The Detectives and then asking us to write a short precis about it afterwards. What I actually did was to practically rewrite the whole story from memory and filled an entire jotter! I recall she made a tremendous fuss of me and I think it was then the seed was sown. If I could get this reaction writing about someone else's work what would it be like to write my own?

For years afterwards I wrote dozens of terrible, silly, short stories that I would read out to anyone who would listen and I remember, even though I was quite shy in those days, that I loved the performance side of it as well.

I was about seven when we moved up to Scotland where dad had been offered a job as a chauffeur/gardener in a little village called Eccles, near Kelso in Roxburghshire.

The teachers at the local school were a husband and wife called Mr and Mrs Elder and although they obviously played their part in furthering my education I have no real outstanding memories about them other than that they were both a bit fierce but Mrs Elder was by far the fiercer!

I also remember that Mr. Elder was the only teacher to have ever used the 'tawse' on me. For those of you who are not familiar with the word it's an instrument of cruelty that used to be allowed in schools – a leather strap that had been cut into strips at one end for maximum effect and that was applied to the hands at very high speed.

I'd also had the pleasure of being caned once at St Joseph's by a wizened, bitter old crone who used to strike fear into the hearts of every child and probably most of the teachers and my crime was being caught talking in the line – those were the days, eh?!

So, from primary school I went on to the Berwickshire High School in Duns and that's where I met Mr Docherty - an Irishman who taught English and who was a complete eccentric! He would stand up in class and get so carried away with his actions while reciting Shakespeare, Dylan Thomas, Burns and Laurie Lee that more than once he knocked over a desk in an empty row causing a domino effect that sent the rest of them crashing and would bring teachers running from all over! He made us laugh a lot but at the same time he lifted those words off the page and brought them to life and we were often spellbound by him.

This man was my other inspiration and I would love to meet him and Miss Varley again. I think they would be quite thrilled to know that they had a hand in my education and I believe they would both love what I'm doing now.

My brother and sister both attended the same schools of course, Mike went straight into the army as a musician in the Kings Own Scottish Borderers for about fifteen years and now works in security and lives near Edinburgh.

My sister, known to most of us as Kat, tried a variety of jobs after leaving school but eventually settled on a career in nursing. She is now married to a farmer, they have two children and live just a few miles outside the village.

When I left school at the age of fifteen I spent about three months at Telford College in Edinburgh learning shorthand and typing but very quickly realised it was not for me. I just could not see myself being someone's secretary for the rest of my days although I had no idea then what I really did want to do as an alternative. However, like my sister, I tried a variety of jobs until I was almost eighteen when I moved to London with a friend.

For the first two years I worked as a residential children's nurse near Crouch End and had some fantastic times with other nurses I met there, as well as a group of lads who shared a flat in Seven Sisters Road, just along from Finsbury Park tube station.

I remember many drunken nights spent with them, either having a party in their flat or spending the evening in one of our favourite pubs such as The Lord Nelson in Holloway Road, The Brecknock in Camden Road or The Flask up in Hampstead.

The children's home was run by a wonderful lady called Matron Levi who was very gruff and down to earth but she cared as much for her nurses as she did for the children.

Sadly the home closed down in the winter of 1975 so we were all made redundant. At that point I came home to stay with my parents for six months, getting a couple of temporary jobs until I decided what to do next.

However, the London 'bug' was still with me and I returned in that famous hot summer of 1976. Initially I stayed with the friends in Seven Sisters Road who very kindly let me use their sofa for a few months then a friend and I eventually got a flat in Archway.

Within a few weeks of my return I got a job as an operator in a communications firm in Vauxhall Bridge Road, Victoria and I enjoyed it so much that I stayed there for the next five years. It was during this time that I also met Dean but you will hear more about that in the next chapter!

My London years were great fun all in all. I was just the right age to appreciate all it had to offer in those days, I enjoyed the hustle and bustle of the city, the night life and the freedom to do whatever I wanted.

Having said that I was still a country girl at heart and on days off I would often head for the nearest park to be among trees and grass. My friend and I spent many happy hours stretched out on the grass up at Alexandra Palace listening to our tinny little radio or rowing round the lake there. More often than not we'd lose an oar and just go round in circles, laughing our heads off and without a care in the world.

They were indeed halcyon days and I'm so grateful for the wonderful memories they've left me with but now that I've lived back in the countryside for twenty years I could not bear to go back to city life again.

I know our children have appreciated living in this kind of environment as well, even though the older ones are now getting itchy feet and beginning to feel a bit stifled.

However, I'm very content to know that wherever they go in the world, whatever career path they follow, they will always be country kids at heart and they will always be able to come home to Moniaive.

Chapter 8

I'm going to get a bit sloppy now because this is where I introduce Dean and the children properly.

Dean and I met on January 8th 1977 and we were introduced through mutual friends who'd met up after not having seen each other for quite some time. Dean's friend invited my pal to a party and she asked if she could bring me along – he agreed because he was going with Dean anyway so they arranged for us all to meet up beforehand.

I clearly recall walking into the room where Dean was lounging across his friend's bed listening to music, he stood up immediately and I couldn't believe how tall he was – his feet touched the floor and the rest of him kept going skywards! I looked at him, saw his lovely gentle eyes and his slow shy smile and at the risk of sounding very corny, my heart was captured.

Mind you, I didn't let him know that for quite a few weeks but he told me later on that it was much the same for him. It appears though that what clinched it for him was when he took me home that night and tried to play a bit of tonsil tennis - I thought he was being too forward so I bit his lip. He tells me that was when he decided I was the girl for him so I suppose you could say it was a slight variation on my mum and her wet dishcloth!

Dean has a wonderful family, most of them are as batty as we are and we've had some fantastic times with them. It would take an entire book on it's own to talk of the mad family parties, the fabulous holidays and the incredible laughs we've had over the years.

They've helped us through our tough times with encouragement and faith and, of course, with humour and we both know that we couldn't have survived without them.

My one regret about being so busy these days is that I don't get to see them very often but I'd like to think I'll be able to take some time off in the fairly near future and try to catch up with them a bit.

However, Dean still gets the chance to pop down several times a year and usually takes one or two of the children with him so at least they are able to see everyone quite regularly.

To get back to Dean for a moment though, we were married in February 1981 so we've been together now for over twenty-four years. We've had some incredibly happy times, we've laughed and cried together and we've been to hell and back because of our financial problems but in all that time there has barely been a cross word between us.

Dean is my hero, my rock and my best friend in the world and there is nothing we can't say to each other. He understands my moods, has the patience of a saint and does most of the cooking and housework these days as well as doing a full time job and I just don't know what I'd do without him.

I should stress here that he is no wimp either, no matter what people may think after such a description. He can't stand the title 'new man' and neither can I – he's not a new man because he's been the way he is all of his life. We love and respect each other, we adore our children, would both do anything for them and we are equals – that's all there is to it.

I should also mention that in the little spare time he has Dean has been heavily involved in youth work for many years. It started about eight years ago when Lee joined the Cubs in a nearby village and Dean offered his services as a helper. It wasn't long before he was 'promoted' to the title of Bagheera and he took the job very seriously – unlike the cubs though because they very quickly started calling him Baggy for short! He has always had a good relationship with youngsters, he's very relaxed with them and they respond well to him, I think they see him more as a friend than a bossy grown up which he appreciates a lot.

A few years ago he also helped to start up a Christian based youth club and although he rarely manages to attend these days I know he would still like to keep in touch with both of these activities whenever possible.

I think that's about all I need to say about Dean for the

moment so now it's time to introduce my children properly, but be warned – some of you might want to get your hankies out quite soon!!

Dean and I moved up to Scotland just a few months after we married and in August of that year we came to live in this area. The first farmhouse we rented was huge and was about seven miles from Moniaive, closer to another village but about two miles up a very narrow, winding country lane. We lived there for eighteen months and had some fantastic times – especially when big groups of friends would come up to visit from London and we'd have some mad parties that often lasted over several days.

My mum and dad came to stay almost every weekend because they loved it here so much and Dean's family came up as often as they could.

They were fabulous days and we have some wonderful memories but none to compare with the day in March 1982 when I phoned the surgery and heard the words "yes Mrs Goddard, your pregnancy test is positive"!

I remember us leaping for joy around the hall for a few minutes, making so much noise that it woke a friend who was staying with us who staggered down the stairs to see what all the fuss was about.

Needless to say our wild parties became much less frequent but we still continued to have a steady stream of visitors throughout that year. I had such a healthy pregnancy that I was quite happy for them to come because most of them were the kind of people who were more than willing to fend for themselves or help with meals and housework anyway. We've had very few people to stay who expect to be waited on hand, foot and finger and if they did they soon got the message!

Anyway, on Saturday 30th October 1982 the great day dawned, ten days later than anticipated therefore I had to be induced, but finally, and after a lot of noise on my part I can tell you, at 7.20pm Jade was born. This little bundle was put into my arms and Dean and I just couldn't speak for emotion. There are no words to describe that sensation of absolute wonder but I clearly remember physically feeling my heart lift from the joy of it.

We could do nothing more than sit and stare at her for what seemed like hours, with her blonde hair, huge brown eyes and lashes so long you could hang your washing on them.

I have to say that the rest of her resembled a pickled walnut at that stage but I'm happy to say she grew out of it!

I recall being wheeled back to my room through the waiting area where my sister and parents were sitting biting their nails for the news. I was as high as a kite from the gas and air I'd been given as well as the euphoria but I was laughing and calling out to them "it was a breeze, no problem" or words to that effect. Needless to say Dean would not have agreed right there and then because he was trying to get the circulation back into his hands from my squeezing them so hard and probably still slightly embarrassed about some of the language I'd used!!

When everyone eventually went home and the nurses finally managed to get me off the ceiling and into bed I spent the entire night just gazing at her. I could not believe how we'd managed to create such a perfect little being and I just couldn't stop thanking God.

We now have three children and I can honestly say that each one's birth was just as unbelievably magical.

Jade is now eighteen of course and very much her own person. She's feisty and proud, intelligent and funny and, as with all of them, there are still days when my heart lifts just to look at her. She recently spent a few months away from home and it was the longest period of time we'd ever been apart in her life so it was very hard for us both. She was actually away at the time of her eighteenth birthday too which was even worse so I sent her this next poem – obviously more personalised so parts of it may only make sense to those who know her but I think you'll understand the sentiment all the same.

MISSING YOU.......

Whenever I find a pair of tights with no holes in the feet!
Whenever I see a block of cheese in the fridge that's been in there for more than two days!
Whenever I see that there are still six packets of Super Noodles a week after we bought them!
Whenever I check the odd socks bag and realise that most of them are yours!
Whenever I open a CD case and find one in there!
Whenever we get the phone bill and find it's been cut by at least a third!
Whenever I hear any one of a dozen records on the jukebox.
Whenever they show 'City of Angels'
Whenever I go into the shed and find it so empty.
Whenever I see pictures of you, at any age, and remember your beautiful eyes and cheeky smile.
Whenever I hear the first line of 'Zoom'.
Whenever I remember the day you were born and knew we'd finally managed to get something right.
Whenever I hear Cyndi Lauper singing 'Come On Home' and wishing that you would.
Whenever I think of you – which is always.

Love you to infinity and way, way beyond.
Mum
October 30th 2000

And that's my girl. We have a great relationship, similar sense of humour, and she has a very kind, caring nature. Having said that, she is a lot like me in that she doesn't suffer fools gladly and if someone upsets or annoys her they'd be well advised to cross the street when they see her coming. To give you a perfect example she loves slogan tee-shirts and one of her favourites says "Warning - this bitch bites"!

She also has my love of words, both reading and writing, is

very artistic, as well as being great with children and she loves to cook , so she has many talents.

As I said earlier we've all had to pitch in together and help a lot since my new venture started. Jade was barely sixteen then but she stepped into my role at home with hardly a murmur, given that she was in her final year at school and she had to cope with all that as well. She took care of the house and especially Rory so much of the time that I don't know how we'd have managed without her.

I don't mean to make it sound as if it's been roses all the way of course, there was a period of adjustment for all of us that was often the cause of arguments between Jade and I but we always managed to get through them and I think it's made us even closer than before. I'm not sure if she'll let me say this bit but there were times at the start when, with her raging hormones and my PMT that it made us mad, bad and dangerous to know but we survived! Suffice to say she has been an absolute diamond, so understanding from the start and so very aware that if I hadn't found this outlet for my emotions that she may well be conversing with me these days through a wire cage!

And now it's time to introduce Lee.

Very soon after Jade was born we realised that we would have to leave our lovely farmhouse because it was no longer practical, it was really far too big and we couldn't afford to keep it heated sufficiently with a new baby in the house.

For the next year or two we stayed in several different places, not quite sure where to settle because at that time Dean didn't have a permanent job but he decided to go to agricultural college which meant us staying with mum and dad again for a while. When his course finished and he'd had no luck getting a job nearby we actually moved back to London for a short while, staying with his family, and intending to find a place out in Oxfordshire so that we would still live in the countryside. However, we never got that far because it was not long before I discovered I was pregnant again and by that time we just knew we had to come 'home' to Dumfriesshire.

Lee was born on 14th April 1985 and as I said before the emotion, the magic and the sheer wonder of it all was just as strong. We had a son. A son who was born with a smile on his face that has been there every day since and who has the ability to make me laugh even when I'm so angry I'm about to burst a blood vessel, or so upset that I'm crying.

He's been there for me so much since this all started and has grown up so fast because of it and again, I don't know what I would have done without him. He's very sensitive to my moods, even though he has days when he's not feeling on top form himself but whenever we argue he's very quick to apologise afterwards.

He's not fond of doing chores as I'm sure he would admit but he realises some days when he comes in from school and I'm standing knee deep in laundry and elbow deep in dishes that it's only fair he does his share. Then he'll feed the animals, take the dog for a walk and ask if there's anything else he can do to help. There was even one occasion when he became my secretary here for a few days!

That happened just after my first article was published and for several days afterwards the phone was ringing off the hook with orders for personalised poems. Fortunately for me it was during the school holidays so Lee came with me to work each day and just answered the phone while I was scribbling away furiously in the corner with a pile of orders beside me.

He was so calm and confident I was amazed, even a reporter who came to interview me for another newspaper remarked on it and asked how long he'd been working for me. She'd made the mistake of thinking he was much older which was easy to understand because, at just fifteen years old, Lee already stands at six foot two in his stocking feet! I should point out that he gets his height from Dean, as does Jade who is about five foot ten, because I am the short-arse of the family at five six! There are times I'm trying to be angry with Jade or Lee and it's almost impossible because I get a crick in my neck looking up at them while I'm shouting and pointing my finger and they just stand there smiling down at me till I think any minute now one of them is going to pat me on the head and say "there, there mum, you can't help being short!"

Lee is continuing to mature steadily but there are times he just wants to mess about like any fifteen year old would. I get cross sometimes when I hear people telling him to act his age because that's exactly what he's doing – again they often make that mistake because of his size. However, he deals with it all in his own way, sometimes he gets annoyed himself but more often than not he just grins his way out of it.

He's also a typical teenage boy in that you can ask him the latest news in football or computer games and he's spot on with them but ask him when he last had a bath or shower and he looks completely baffled!

There was a time in his early teens that he went through a spell of being very unsure of himself, much the same as most youngsters of that age. Because he has such an easy going nature he was happy to be friends with everyone but occasionally his peers would try to make him choose between them or just give him a hard time some days.

However, he doesn't care much at all these days about what they think and if they don't like it then it's just tough luck as far as he's concerned. He also gets on with all age groups, is very comfortable in the company of adults and has a wicked sense of humour that often gets him into trouble as well as out of it!

He and Jade both have a lot of respect for my dad and get on really well with him so Lee often goes round to sit with his grandad and listen to his army tales and stories about his youth but with my dad's hearing problem their conversations can be quite hilarious at times. So there you have it, he's my gentle giant and I love him to bits!

By the time Rory was born in 1993 we had been suffering financially for many years, Dean's first business had failed in the mid 1980's and we were still paying off the debts. We hadn't intended to extend the family, especially since we had one of each, but in March of that year I got confirmation that I was pregnant again and at first we were stunned. With all the stress we'd been under for so long we just weren't sure how we would cope and I worried throughout most of my pregnancy that I might feel differently about this baby.

Apart from anything else Jade and Lee had both been such fantastic babies, sleeping through the night from the age of six weeks, walking and talking very quickly and both out of nappies by the age of two so I just couldn't convince myself I could be that lucky again.

However, from the very second they placed Rory in my arms and I gazed down on his face I knew everything was going to be fine. I was only in hospital for two days but I remember often sitting cross legged on the bed, with him lying in front of me and I just couldn't stop looking at him – several nurses used to comment on the fact that sometimes I wouldn't move for hours.

Quite a few times during my pregnancy I'd questioned why God had apparently given us this extra burden to deal with but every time I gazed upon this beautiful child in those first few days I knew why - he had been sent to us as a gift.

From the moment he was born he lightened all our lives and has continued to do so ever since. He very definitely saved my sanity and I'm sure Dean would agree that he saved his. Jade was eleven by then and Lee was eight and they adored him. They quickly learned how to hold him and feed him and would do anything for him, so much so that it was almost as though Rory had four parents instead of two.

I did get away with it a third time as well because he was sleeping through the night in no time and continued to develop just as quickly as the other two - he's now seven and in his third year at school which he thoroughly enjoys and seems to be coping with very well. He is also very mature for his age, especially in his speech which can cause a lot of hilarity – he sometimes sounds like a wise little old man and often creases us up with the things he says.

He's sensitive and kind and so polite and well behaved that

he rarely has to be told off but on the occasions he does he just looks back at you, all wide eyed and sad and you just can't help wanting to hug him. A good friend recently said something that sums him up very well because she was in the shop one day and got talking to Rory for quite a while then when she was about to leave she remarked that she could just squeeze him till his eyes popped out! It caused Rory to look a bit alarmed for a moment but I knew what she meant because he has that effect on me every time I see him.

By November 1998 Rory had been attending Sunday School for quite a while so we often used to have little chats about God. The following poem was inspired by a conversation I had with him very early one morning when he trotted out in bare feet and pyjamas to sit with me on the garden wall where I was having a cup of tea:

FOR RORY

My son told me "God is in everything"
And I answered him "really, my dear?"
He was patient and spoke to me slowly
He is very advanced for five years.

He proceeded to tell me the next bit
"God's even in raspberries and grass"
So I thought and I pondered and realised
He was right, so then why did I ask

"Do you think he's in us then, my darling?"
And he fixed me with a withering stare
"But of course mum, we're all God's children"
To argue with that I don't dare.

> Then I looked at the clock, then at Rory
> Who was about to say more to explain
> "Now this could be a long conversation"
> I thought, as he sat down again.
>
> So I stopped him and pointed out gently
> It was late, he was only half-dressed
> Then as we ran up the lane for the school bus
> I thanked God for my son – I am blessed.

You might not be surprised to hear that this was one of my best sellers in individual form on the stall and it sold even more copies when Rory was there to help me because he would point it out to people and they just couldn't resist him.

So those are my children. They are individual in so many ways and yet so alike and my life revolves around them still. Even though I have to spend so much time in the shop nowadays they are always in my thoughts and I love them all so much that sometimes it hurts.

They are with me all the way in what I'm doing now and realise that at the end of the day it's all for them. I'm constantly being told that what I do is brilliant, that I have a gift and that my venture is very unique but I don't consider myself anything special – I'm just a mum with a mission!

Chapter 9

Now at this point I suppose I should explain a bit more about how we came to settle here in this village and why there is nowhere else on earth I would rather live. In time to come I'd like to think that we will be in a position to travel abroad on holiday for a few weeks, maybe even months, but I will always have the comforting knowledge that I will eventually come 'home' to Moniaive.

There are many reasons for thinking of it as home but one of the most important ones for me is that we have been in this area for almost twenty years now which is the longest I have stayed anywhere and it means that at last I have roots.

As I explained in the chapter about my parents our family moved many times throughout my childhood, starting in England and then moving to Scotland, because we had to go wherever my dad could get work.

However, even though I chose to live in London when I was older I still loved coming back to stay with my parents at every opportunity. I would even save up days off so that I could squeeze in an extra little holiday every few weeks because I could only go for so long without smelling the sweet Scottish air.

Initially I used to come home by train but when I met Dean he was driving for a living so at least once a month we'd point the van northwards and bomb up the motorway to Dechmont in West Lothian.

Dean always loved Scotland so when we did marry and thought about starting a family we were determined our children would not be raised in a city environment and it seemed perfectly natural that we should move up here.

I've already mentioned the fact that we came to live in this area to start with, moved away again for a short spell and then came back because we just knew this was where we were meant to be.

Our children were all born here, they consider themselves to be Scottish and they are very proud of it. Now I know that there are a handful of people in this village who resent anyone who was not born and bred here, and especially the English. They dislike the fact that there are so many of us 'incomers' now but my response to that is they should be pleased and proud to know that it is such a wonderful place to live, which is why we're all here.

The majority of people are warm, welcoming and friendly and quite happy for us to be here – they realise too that if it weren't for all the new people moving into the area the village might have 'died' a long time ago. We have brought custom for local shops and hotels and children for the school, we use local tradesmen wherever possible and some of us have started businesses that have attracted visitors and tourists, thereby bringing more revenue into the community. Most of us are involved in village life, whether it's the PTA, gala committee, local council, youth club, brownies and guides or whatever – you name it and we're on it!

The reason for this is that we care very much about the community and want to keep it a decent, safe place for our children. We want the shops and schools to remain open and thriving and we want to help improve certain things over a period of time so that when our children are older there is housing and employment for them. That way they may not find it necessary to move away because there is nothing here for them. We want them to have a future here, in this friendly little corner of South West Scotland.

So to anyone who resents us I would say that whatever name they call us by, be it incomers, foreigners, white settlers or any other description, the fact is we mean no-one any harm and we are here to stay.

I recently heard of a man who used to live here, sadly he is no longer alive, called David Logan-Brown and I'm told he was quite a character.

He was born in India to a wealthy tea planting family but was educated in Scotland and the reason he came to my attention was that someone was kind enough to hand in a poem he had written for a competition that he'd won first prize for.

Although the contest was to commemorate the centenary of the building of the Forth Railway Bridge, his theme was along the lines that Scotland should be building a bridge towards friendship with her neighbours. He wrote the original poem in Scots but with an English translation. It says almost exactly what I have just said, it is a fantastic poem and I would love to be able to trace his family to get permission to print it. I've since been shown several newspaper articles about him as well as another of his poems and I really regret not having had the privilege to have met him all those years ago – I think we might well have struck up quite a friendship!

So as you can tell I'm enjoying life immensely now, every day is different and I never know what to expect when I come in to the shop each morning.

There was a time I could go for several days without seeing anyone or folk would rush in just to say hello and rush out again very quickly but for quite a while now it's been busy every day with people calling in and often staying for hours.

More often than not I'm quite happy to join in with their conversations and ignore my work because fortunately it's something I can catch up on anywhere and at any time, so there are occasions when I'm in the shop all day and I don't write a word!

However lately, especially now that I've decided to get a move on with this book, I find that I can sit down at the computer and start typing and very soon I'm lost in what I'm doing and completely oblivious to what's going on around me.

The good thing is that most of my regular visitors recognise the signs now and they all just get on and talk to each other without disturbing me – half the time I'm not even aware of their conversations.

A friend recently suggested as a joke that I should get myself a big pair of fluffy earmuffs with a sign saying that if I'm wearing them no one should attempt to talk to me. The trouble is I look manic enough when I'm writing, with my glazed expression, tongue sticking out slightly and usually a pen stuck behind my ear that the addition of earmuffs would probably frighten away the tourists or have me carted off to the local funny farm!

My family are also used to me living on a different planet these days, they think it's very funny a lot of the time and they are so supportive about what I'm doing. I'm fairly sure that Jade and Lee secretly think it's cool to have a batty mother – in fact Jade once looked me straight in the eye and said "you're not quite normal are you mum?." It's one of the nicest things anyone's ever said to me!

Seriously though, they are all beginning to take it in their stride and they try to help out whenever they can. Both the elder ones help me a lot with Rory, Lee will babysit and Jade will read to him and entertain him as often as possible. I think they both appreciate that his childhood is very different to their own when I was always at home for them so they help to keep things as normal as they can for him. It's a great relief to me, although I'm pleased to say the shop is only a few hundred yards from his school so I'm never very far away from him. The shop is also so cosy and comfortable that it's like a home from home anyway and they all enjoy being here, especially through the holidays.

Dean makes a point of spending a lot of time with Rory at weekends because he often has to stay away a few nights through the week and since I try to have the shop open every day it gives them a chance to catch up with each other.

Truth to tell it's very difficult to get me out of the shop these days and for a long time now Dean has been doing the food shop every week because I can't stand doing it any more.

There was a time when I was quite happy to stroll round the supermarket for hours, poring over the bargains and just taking my time. Nowadays though I think of it as an irritating chore that keeps me from my work and I get so impatient that Dean and the others have practically ordered me to leave them to it from now on.

Apart from anything else I am so easily distracted, especially if I'm thinking about ideas for my book, that according to them I'm not safe to be let out on my own. Just recently I attempted to accompany Dean round Tesco's, went off in search of a jar of gherkins and he didn't see me again for about half an hour!

Still, it doesn't bother me and as long as they can live with it that's fine. Occasionally I'll have moments of lucidity and become quite focussed on what's going on around me but it doesn't happen very often and it only startles them anyway.

The rest of our family and friends have also begun to adjust to the complete change in me and they realise it's something I've needed for a very long time and that I just have to do it. They've always known of my love of writing and they were all very worried about me at times during the worst of our money problems so I know that they're happy for me now, even if they were a bit anxious when I first started.

I think that was because once my new venture began I was on such an emotional high all the time they were worried that if things didn't work out I would come crashing down to earth so heavily that I might never recover so now and then they tried to hang on to my ankles to stop me from flying too high!

I owe every one of them so much for their continued support that I hardly know where to begin to thank them. Over the years they have helped us out in so many ways, not just financially but with encouragement, hugs and even prayers - without them we would have surely crumbled and we owe them an enormous debt of gratitude.

Another thing that helped Dean and I through our darkest days was that we never lost our faith, even though we both dealt with it in different ways.

Although I was brought up as a Catholic and regularly went to Mass and confession until the age of about seven, when we moved up here we attended our local Church of Scotland.

Mum had been brought up quite strictly in the Catholic

faith I believe, but in later years had dropped away so she and dad seldom went to church and he left it to her to decide on our behalf. When we came to Scotland we carried on by attending Sunday School at the local village church but by our mid teens we'd all fallen by the wayside, so to speak.

Dean on the other hand was brought up in The Salvation Army, his family having been connected to it for generations, but by the age of about fifteen he decided to leave. From then on he had no real wish or desire to attend any church, although he always kept his faith. It was not until our present minister came here six years ago that he felt here was someone he liked and respected enough to persuade him back to the church.

Needless to say his return to the church was around the same time we had reached one of the lowest ebbs in our financial despair and for that reason I was very happy for him to have found something to give him more strength.

Although I had always kept my faith I did not yet feel strong enough to go back to church and face people. There were many times during those years when I'd had reason to doubt God's existence, especially when mum died, which also coincided with the start of our financial problems. I'm happy to say that despite all that, and especially with what has happened to me over the past two years, I am now of the opinion that he is definitely up there!

Again I think I have our friend Christine, the minister, to thank for a lot of that because she has been so kind, supportive and understanding. Even though I still don't attend church regularly, she knows that I talk to God a lot, whether it's here in the shop, out in the garden or even on one of my rare trips round Tesco's - I don't have to ask him for anything much these days because I know things will be fine from now on but I just like to keep him up to date.

Chapter 10

OK that's enough of the serious stuff for now, I think it's time for another couple of poems. I'm fairly sure the next one was the first I ever wrote, also one of the longest, round about 1990, and it's one of two in similar vein about a typical day in the life of a mum. It starts with a dream sequence in the Garden of Eden and should also let you see that once upon a time I did have a fairly routine and organised life – albeit harassed at times!

ONE DAY IN THE LIFE

The sun is so warm, the heaven's so blue
And Adam is reaching for me
When above him I saw a huge spider
Suspended from our special tree.

I reached up to dust off the cobwebs
And knocked off an apple, which fell
Then suddenly bells started ringing
Damn the alarm clock – oh well!

Stagger from bed to the bathroom
Warm splash and teeth quickly brushed
Wake husband and children who grumble
They really don't like being rushed.

Downstairs now and deftly avoiding
The skateboards, the dog and the cat
Switch on kettle and grill, check for letters
Two bills and one very wet mat!

The cat, now disgraced, is ejected
Make tea, check the cereal packet
Hide plastic toy before children come down
No toy – no debate – so no racket!

Bread under grill, set the table
Shout up the stairs – final warning
Four faces appear looking wary
They don't mess with mum in the morning!

House silent, start rounding up laundry
Do dishes, make beds, quickly dust
Hoover the carpet then out to the car
Good grief, what a bucket of rust!

Top speed round the shop with a trolley
That veers left when I want to go right
Home again, start thinking of dinner
Should I make a lasagne tonight?

All done, time to spare, soak in bathtub
Milkman rings, start searching for purse
Step in something disgusting the dog did
Cat pardoned, dog exiled, sin worse!

Meal over, kids bathed and in bed now
Hubby has his post-prandial nap
I'm feeling quite drowsy, a howl makes us jump
The dog's wedged herself in the cat flap!

I'm back in the Garden of Eden once more
Farewell to all trouble and sorrow
Here's Adam again, he's one hell of a hunk
But I must wash his fig leaf tomorrow!!

The next one is along very similar lines and I sent a copy of it to Dr Hilary Jones of GMTV because I happened to hear him mention that he supported a baby charity with the same name as the title of my poem. I received a nice letter back from him to say that he and his wife had enjoyed it and it had really made them laugh because they could identify with it themselves having three small children of their own. You will have gathered that most of my poems so far have been four line verses, this is one of the few that has six.

BLISS

I've got the Monday morning blues
I decided with a sigh
Even the baby doesn't seem to be too happy
As I picked her up to cuddle her
I could smell the reason why
She had done a little parcel in her nappy.

Then my toddler gave a yell
Oh damn, I forgot about him
I'd left him in the bathroom on the potty
He'd been shoving the cat down the toilet
Just to see if it could swim
Now it staggered past me looking dazed and grotty.

I offered up a prayer for strength
Just to get me through the day
And dreamt again of a villa in Corfu
Then came back to earth with a vengeance
As I heard my daughter say
That the baby's face was a funny shade of blue.

Having dealt with that little crisis
I put the young ones down to sleep
And decided what I needed was a bath
I filled the tub with foaming water,
Checked the babies – not a peep
Then jumped into the bubbles with a splash.

I felt the tension drain away
As I laid back with a sigh
And thought things weren't so dreadful after all
Till the phone rang, then the doorbell
I heard the baby start to cry
And the sound of little footsteps in the hall.

I grabbed a towel, got quickly dressed
And ran to open the door
To find a lady from Barnardo's with a tin
Whoever rang had just hung up
The cat had piddled on the floor
And my son was wearing nothing but a grin.

It's ten o'clock, there's peace at last
I check the children once again
And as I watch their little bodies warm and curled
I think back on the day and smile
Knowing tomorrow will be the same
But I wouldn't swop my 'angels' for the world!

Again that was written in 1990 which was several years before Rory came along so perhaps I had an instinct about a third child – even though I got the gender wrong!

Chapter 11

I suppose now that all of my family have been mentioned this might be a good time to talk about the other members of our household so here come the pets!

We have a cat called Cinders who is about fifteen now and she's also one of the stroppiest animals I've ever come across. The only one she has any time for is Jade, who more or less claimed her from the start, and she leads the dogs a hell of a life. She's also a pain in the neck in the mornings because the second she hears anyone moving about she literally yells for her breakfast. More often than not we just feed her to shut her up but some days we make her wait, depending on how long we can stand the noise.

Our oldest dog is Sophie, a grand old dame who has reached the age of sixteen which we're told is pretty remarkable for a Great Dane, I think that makes her about a hundred and twelve in human years! She was a rescue dog and only about two when we got her so she was very lively then although of course she's very slow and shaky on her pins now. I still recall the day Dean took her out for a run in the field just after we got her - she'd been charging around for a while and had gathered such momentum that when she ran up behind Dean and rammed into him, such was her size and strength that she literally lifted him off his feet and carried him for a few yards!

The funniest thing about her though is that, despite her size, she's always been a craven coward and has made us laugh on many occasions because of it. I've lost count of the times a balloon's been burst, a door has slammed unexpectedly or someone has shouted suddenly and she has practically hyperventilated. Despite this though she's been a very special part of our family for a long time now and has always been protective of us, especially me because she was so sensitive to my moods when I used to get the blues a lot.

Now we turn to Rhubarb. What can I tell you about this mad young dog and where do I start?! She came into our lives in May 1999, another rescue dog, also a Great Dane, who I was foolish enough to agree to take on after a night in the pub with the very same lady who led us to Sophie all those years ago! She was only five months old when we first brought her home and had spent her life up to then outside and in a kennel. Oh, how I wish we'd continued with her that way!

The day we brought her home she was so terrified about coming into the house that Dean had to lift her up and even then she splayed all four legs in the doorway to stop us getting her through it! For the first few weeks we kept her in the kitchen when we had to go out because we decided it was the one room where she could do least damage. How wrong can you be?! I returned home one day to find that not only had she knocked several plates off the draining board which were smashed but she'd managed to nudge the cupboard open where I kept all my baking ingredients. Have you any idea how much area one bag of flour can cover? Added to that there were also several unmentionable heaps dotted around which, as you can imagine from their size, our dogs manage to produce regularly, and on a par with a Clydesdale horse!

Rhubarb is also as cowardly as Sophie and for some reason seems to be afraid of men, older men in particular, so it makes things a bit tricky when Jade or Lee try to take her for a walk through the village. She has to be practically dragged along and whenever she sees a man she cringes and shakes but growls at the same time which can be embarrassing. It must look awful to other people who don't know her story, they may well even think that we're responsible for her behaviour which upsets me as well. On the other hand however if they walk her in the other direction, out of the village towards the fields, she obviously senses where she's going and takes off like an Exocet missile with Jade or Lee tearing along behind in a cloud of dust and with their trainers practically smouldering!

There was a time that Sophie and Cinders used to have a love/hate relationship and didn't get on at all but I think they must have come to an agreement as they got older to ignore each other, so nowadays Cinders takes her spite out on Rhubarb. Very often she lies in wait somewhere, ready to pounce at the first opportunity, causing Rhubarb to have an attack of the vapours and require resuscitation.

So that's our animals – all completely mad and therefore very well suited to our household! I've written a poem each for Cinders and Sophie, before Rhubarb came to stay but I also wrote one a long time ago that was one of the few that aren't actually completely true about us – the only verse that really applies is the last one.

THE MENAGERIE

There's a pot-bellied pig in our garden
And a guinea pig out in the shed
They wanted a boa constrictor
But they got a nice grass snake instead.

There are hamsters and rabbits and gerbils
And they all have babies of course
In the field down below there's a donkey
As well as a knackered old horse.

There's a lovely old cow called Cassandra
With her calf and a couple of sheep
And an ancient old bull with a prostate
Who has long since stopped earning his keep.

We have tadpoles and frogs and some goldfish
A canary, a budgie, a parrot
There's also a goat christened Albert
Who'll oblige with a kiss for a carrot.

Now that covers all of the livestock
That I and my husband sustain
Unless you include our three children
And our cat and neurotic Great Dane!

In actual fact this was written with our mad pal Jane in mind – she runs a small animal sanctuary just outside the village and she lives and works for them. Whenever there's a local event, no matter how small, Jane will be there on her stall come rain or shine raising funds for her animals. She can have the strangest mixture there at any one time and I've always had a suspicion she has an ark hidden away round the back somewhere.

It was thanks to her we acquired our dogs as well, a fact that I'm never sure we should thank her for or not because unfortunately both dogs also have a flatulence problem that must be doing serious damage to the ozone layer. It's quite a common occurrence in the evenings for the whole family to be sitting watching telly with our jumpers pulled up to just below our eyes to block out the smell! Still we're stuck with them now, with all their strange and funny ways and I just couldn't imagine life without them.

Chapter 12

I mentioned earlier about having done a couple of poetry reading evenings in the past year. The very fact that I can say I've done them is an indication of how much my confidence has grown because I could never have imagined myself doing such a thing at the start. The idea was first suggested to me by a man called Dudley Russell, the husband and manager of Pam Ayres, after I'd written to tell him about what I was doing and asking his advice about what to do next.

I should think it's quite obvious why I chose him because my humorous poems had often been likened to his wife's style He replied with a very nice long letter, congratulating me on the idea and wishing me luck but he also suggested, not surprisingly I suppose, that I should think about doing public readings, he even suggested a venue not far from here that had a capacity of about 200.

I must admit that when I first read his letter I almost instantly dismissed the idea because I really couldn't see myself ever having the nerve to do such a thing. However, over a period of time it occurred to me that I'd actually been doing it on a very small scale anyway, both in the shop to several customers and in the pub. I would sometimes be asked to read them to a group of three or four people there and have others listening in around us.

Anyway I finally decided to have a go but felt I'd be more comfortable with just friends and family the first time so I used the dining room of the pub and asked about fifteen to twenty people along. Although most of them were familiar with a lot of my work they still thoroughly enjoyed it, especially when I told a little story about each one first.

I was slightly nervous to begin with but they were so appreciative that it didn't take long for me to relax. The next venue I chose some months later was at The Artist's Café in Dumfries, owned by a great couple called Carol and Mark who I met when they came into the shop last summer. They had been told about me by someone and were intrigued enough to come and see what it was all about – since then we've become good friends and they've been very supportive and encouraging, making me welcome in their café whenever I go into town.

The reading I did there had been advertised for a week or so in advance and there were quite a few new faces so it was a bit more nerve racking but I enjoyed it all the same. It also helped that my dad was there and because of his hearing problem he kept muttering quite loudly so after a while I announced to the audience, a lot of whom had no idea who he was, that I'd hired him from Rent-a-Heckler!

I felt the night went well, although there may have been one or two people who'd come along expecting more 'arty farty' poetry but they seemed to enjoy it all the same. I might consider doing it again at some time in the future but for the moment I'm just happy to have tried it and I still get the opportunity to do it to small groups quite regularly.

I have made an effort to tear myself away from the village a bit more often in the past few months, especially if I can get someone to watch the shop, but sometimes I even close it for the day and take myself off to The Artist's Café.

I lug my huge briefcase along with me and just settle myself down at a table and work away, being supplied regularly with pots of tea. Again I have to confess that I sometimes don't get any work done at all because I go in with friends and we get talking to Carol and Mark as well as their other customers but at least it gives me a break now and then.

Although the shop is much busier these days there are still quiet spells so I sometimes just go along to the pub to work. It's especially nice through the winter months when they usually have a lovely big fire on so it saves my electricity and gas bills as well!

The landlady even lets me take my lap top along and the regulars are getting used to seeing me working in there. Sometimes visitors are even intrigued enough to ask what I'm doing and we get into conversations about it, this is often when I'm asked to read some of my poems and I've even been known to sell a booklet or two at the same time.

A lot of these visitors are so enchanted by the village, how pretty it is and how friendly and welcoming the people are that many times they do stay a few hours longer than they intended. Some have been known to book into the hotel and stay several days and a lot of them have come back again on several occasions.

Again I'll say it's not perfect because we are only human so there are upsets and silly squabbles between folk now and then but as far as I'm concerned it's the nearest place to heaven on earth I've ever known.

My outlook on life and the human race in general is a very simple one and it's coming up next – one of the rare pieces I've written that doesn't rhyme.

PHILOSOPHY OF LIFE – "I understand"

Treat every single person in life as an equal. Think of them as no better or worse than you are, no matter what age, colour, religion, disability etc and be prepared, even if you think you hate them, to step into their shoes for a moment. You may then understand why that person is doing something that you think is wrong. No-one in this world is any better or worse than you are. They have simply been dealt a hand of cards in life and they are playing those cards to the best of their ability to achieve what they think is best for them. If you do take the time to step into their shoes you would understand why they are doing what they think is right with the cards they have been dealt. You may not agree with them, but you would understand.

If every person reading this were to go out and tell someone else and those people told others it would take a very short time for the message to spread. Then all of those people could step into those other shoes and understand. Then they might think "right – I see it from their side now – so what can we do about it?"

That's the first time I've read that piece in many months and on reflection it's not that well written, a bit repetitive and some people will think it's quite pompous. Why should I think my philosophy is anything special? The fact is I don't – it's a philosophy that's been said and written many thousands of different ways from biblical times to present day.

What I'm trying to say is that we do all deserve to be treated with the same respect, no matter how lowly our position in life and if we just take the time to try and imagine how it is for others it would make it so much easier for us all to get along.

It doesn't mean you should interfere in peoples lives or offer help where it's not wanted but sometimes all it takes is a smile or a kind word to make them feel better and it costs nothing.

Some people are very private about themselves and are not comfortable discussing their business – I understand that perfectly and wouldn't dream of imposing. On the other hand I can often sense that they'd like to talk, not necessarily in great detail and sometimes not about their problems at all – all they want to do is relax, have a chat and forget about other stuff for a while.

I know I'm becoming more intuitive these days and I do try to be friendly to everyone but it's not always easy. There are also times I get told off by family and friends for worrying too much about others but I can't help it – unless someone is really obnoxious or nasty I just like to help where I can.

When I think back on how I used to be I often cringe at my insensitivity. A lot of the time I assumed a hard, kind of "so what, we've all got problems – get over it" attitude or sometimes I was so lost in my own worry and self pity I wouldn't even notice theirs and I hadn't the mental or physical strength to help them anyway.

I've been told many times since I started this business that I have a 'gift' and although at first I wouldn't accept it I know now that it is the case. It's given me the opportunity to help other people and I've had so much fun and pleasure with it because it's cleared my once-foggy mind and enabled me to put my own problems in perspective.

That's not to say that my mind doesn't still get foggy these days of course – there can be a real pea-souper in there at times because I often have so many things to do at once that I run around like a headless chicken all day and end up getting nothing done at all!

The difference is that most of it is enjoyable and on days like these there are often friends in the shop who help me and we can always find something to laugh about along the way.

I'm hopelessly disorganised when it comes running a business – I hate all the 'bumph' you have to deal with like keeping accounts and so on and I wish I could afford to employ someone really efficient to do it for me. Some days my friends or Jade will come in and try to have a sort out for me but it's such an unbelievable muddle it's impossible to know where to start so they often give up in despair. The truth I just don't want to do it, it irritates me beyond belief because all I want to do is write.

I'm sure the time will come when I'll be in a position to take someone on to deal with all the background stuff and I pity them already when I think of the mess they'll have to start with but for the moment I'm happy just to muddle along with things as they are.

Chapter 13

Last year I had the great pleasure and privilege of attending a seminar in Glasgow called Women In Business 2000 and it was one of the most inspiring days of my life. There were over 1300 of us there and by the end of it almost every woman must have left feeling they could conquer the world!

The whole event was run so professionally but in such a friendly manner that you couldn't help but feel at ease and enjoy yourself. The four women speakers were all so gutsy, so funny and so all round entertaining that we were spellbound when they spoke.

However, the one who stood out for me (and obviously many others because she received a standing ovation) was a lovely young girl called Heather Mills.

Now I knew a fair amount about Heather from reading about her in magazines and seeing her on TV a few times over the years and had always admired her courage but I had no idea how much of her story I was not aware of. As a lot of people will know she has been a model for a long time and was involved in a tragic freak accident where she lost her leg.

This was the one thing that almost everyone was aware of because Heather had made a point of being very public about it afterwards to let people know how she'd coped with it and to inspire others in similar circumstances not to give up hope. She had also become involved in working with people in war torn countries who had lost limbs and has campaigned strongly to get artificial limbs for them.

What I did not know was about her life prior to the accident and it was when she told us this part that many of us were moved to tears. This young woman stood in front of us and told us everything. She spoke of her life from the age of nine and it was heart-rending but at the same time she often made it hilariously funny. Even the story of the day she lost her leg had us in stitches! If I had to find a complaint about that day the only thing I could come up with is that we should have been supplied with tissues before she started to speak. She was wonderful. So refreshingly honest and open without a hint of being a martyr or looking for sympathy, she just tells it like it is and was.

I was told afterwards that she now has a very famous boyfriend but as much as I admire him I get irritated when I hear people refer to her as 'Paul McCartney's girlfriend'.

That may be so but as I am always quick to point out she was wealthy and famous long before she met him and should be recognised for her humanitarian work and as a person in her own right and I'm quite sure Sir Paul would agree with my sentiments himself.

There were so many things she said that echoed what I am trying to do and I think if I ever have the pleasure of meeting her in person she would probably realise that although I am older, greyer and more wrinkled I am also a kindred spirit!

You will have gathered by now that I am easily moved in a lot of situations, both happy and sad ones and for that reason you won't be surprised to hear that I have shed quite a few tears since I started writing this story. The fact is I think tears are a wonderful form of release and they don't embarrass me at all, whether they're mine or anyone else's. I think of them as a safety valve for when emotions are running too high and if we couldn't cry sometimes there would be a lot more of us meeting up in the funny farm instead of here in the shop!

On several occasions friends have come in to find me sitting here at the computer with tears pouring down my face but it doesn't trouble them at all. They know there's nothing to worry about on my behalf so they just carry on talking to each other in the background as if nothing was wrong.

I'm going to introduce a few words written by other people that have inspired me throughout this venture and some from even before that. I'm sure everyone will have read or heard a phrase or story at some time in their lives that just seemed so appropriate for what is happening to them at that moment and they remember it for a very long time. Not surprisingly there are dozens of them for me! One of the most recent ones was in a book given to me by great friends to celebrate the first anniversary of the shop opening, it was full of quotes about women, mainly by women, and this one just leapt off the page when I read it, written by a lady called Pam Brown

"No-one should be surprised if the woman next door suddenly goes off to climb Everest or sail round the world – she just washed one plate too many!"

No prizes for guessing why that one appealed to me!

I've mentioned several times how much our family and friends have helped us in the past and how supportive they've been in many different ways. They were always thinking of us and constantly trying to find ways to let us know this – very often by sending us cards they'd found with appropriate words in them and this next one was sent to us by Dean's aunt several years ago.

Remember when cares overtake you
And you're waiting for grey skies to clear
That life is a series of changes
And a brighter tomorrow is near
That each day is a brand new beginning
Each day has a bright new dawn
So when you come to the end of your rope
Tie a knot in the end and hang on!

That was a humorous example but the next one, also sent by the same lady, is in a more serious vein.

We said a prayer for you today
We know God must have heard
We felt the answer in our hearts
Although he spoke no word
We did not ask for wealth or fame
(We knew he wouldn't mind)
We asked instead for treasures
Of a far more different kind
We asked that he'd be near you
At the start of each new day
To grant you health and happiness
And friends to share your way
We asked for blessings for you
In all things great and small
But it was for his loving care
We prayed for most of all.

And, as you will have gathered, those prayers have been answered.

This one was sent by my brother Mike who has also been very supportive and he too has a love of words. He collects phrases and stories that he writes down in a book and I often get phone calls from him just to read one out to me.

Build for yourself a strongbox
Fashion each part with care
When it's as strong as your hands can make it
Put all your troubles in there
Hide there all thoughts of your failures
And each bitter cup that you've quaffed
Lock all your heartaches within it
Then sit on the lid and laugh!

And as far as I'm concerned I've been sitting on that strongbox for quite some time now and I've been laughing ever since!

My brother also sent me this next one about three years ago. I mentioned that he'd been a musician in the army but since leaving he has continued with his music in a TA band. He found these words whilst looking through some old music scores and just knew we'd love them. I've already made reference to the grotty old farmhouse we lived in before we moved into the village (more details about that at a later date, I think!) and Dean's job involves a lot of driving and having to spend nights away from home so you'll understand why this moved him quite a lot when he first read it.

LITTLE GREY HOME IN THE WEST

When the golden sun sinks in the hills
And the toil of a long day is o'er –
Though the road may be long, in the lilt of a song
I forget I was weary before.
Far ahead, where the blue shadows fall
I shall come to contentment and rest
And the toils of the day will be all charmed away
In my little grey home in the west.
There are hands that will welcome me in
There are lips I am burning to kiss
There are two eyes that shine just because they are mine
And a thousand things other men miss
It's a corner of heaven itself
Though it's only a tumble-down nest
But with love brooding there why no place can compare
With my little grey home in the west.

D. EARDLEY-WILMOT

I wept buckets when I first read that and it still moves me to this day. My sister Kat sneaked it away for a few days and put it in a beautiful silver frame for Dean's birthday, naturally it has pride of place in the sitting room.

By now you will have realised what a fantastic, loving family we both have and you will understand how we managed to survive so far. In their own ways they have also worried about me since I started this business because a lot of the time I was on such an emotional high that it must have at first appeared that I was actually heading for a breakdown. I'm still as high as a kite most days, but it's from pure happiness and I very definitely don't need any pills for it! There are days when I stop long enough to worry about the bills for the shop that I can't really afford to pay, I am struggling to keep up with them I have to admit but I am so convinced that what I'm writing now is going to solve those problems that it doesn't trouble me for long. I've seen the reactions of over four hundred people to the first draft, on several occasions I've watched three or four of them all reading it at the same time and they've been completely engrossed. I've watched them smile, heard them laugh and I've even seen some of them reach for a hanky so I know this is it – it's what I was born to do and I feel so privileged to know how much it's been appreciated.

Almost every day now I have friends in the shop who make me laugh so much that my ribs are aching by the time I go home – in their own ways they're all causing ripples too, whether they realise it or not, and I have to pinch myself some days because I can't believe how lucky I am to have found a job that gives me so much pleasure. I thank God for it almost daily as well, usually at night when my brain still won't switch off because it's so full of ideas. He's a great boss, I love the working conditions and the pay is potentially fantastic but I must have a word with him about the hours!

Chapter 14

OK, enough of the inspirational stuff for now. There will be more of it to come of course but let's get back to the subject of the village again. You already know how much I love the place and how highly I think of most of the people, and although I know there are many who think I'm definitely a bit wacky I'm sure they know I'm harmless.

There are occasions when I wander out of the shop with my mind on a few dozen other things and I look quite vague and distracted, sometimes muttering to myself, or I'll suddenly remember something I need and do a quick about turn to get it. I don't do it deliberately of course and I expect people are beginning to get used to it by now but once in a while something happens to make me realise just how odd I must look to others, especially strangers.

A good example of this is that I have been known to talk to a Post Office mailbox!

Now this might strike you as really bizarre but there is a perfectly reasonable explanation. As you can appreciate a great deal of my work comes and goes through the mail and for that reason I spend a lot of time in the Post Office. The couple who run it, Sharon and Paul have been very encouraging and supportive of my venture from the start although I'm sure they must have wondered, among many others, what the hell I was actually trying to do at the beginning.

Sharon helped me a lot with furnishing and fittings when I first opened and still continues to let me know if she hears of anything that might be of use in the shop and her husband Paul also runs his own desk top publishing business. He prints a lot of my stationery, headed paper, compliments slips, business cards etc as well as doing all my laminating because he has all the fancy machinery required so again I have a great deal to thank them for. You can imagine how much easier it makes my life to have all this literally on the doorstep because I shudder to think how I'd have managed if I'd had to trek into the nearest town every time I needed to use the postal service. Consequently there are days when I'm in and out of there at least half a dozen times. However, there have been times when I've needed a quick bit of advice and the Post Office is closed but I know they're still in there, cashing up or whatever – so I just have a chat through the mail box! It seems perfectly natural to me and I never think to look around and see if anyone's watching me but on occasion strangers have been driving by and either slowed down and looked at me in astonishment or alternately have put their foot to the floor and burnt rubber all the way up the High Street! And that's what these poor villagers have to put up with at times so it's no wonder I still get odd looks from some of them.

Sharon and Paul also know my dad very well of course, they recognise his moods and they treat him accordingly but he has a great relationship with them all in all and he thinks the world of them. The next poem was inspired by an incident that happened in November 1998 and the lady in question is the one I've just been talking about.

THE LOST PENGUIN

My dad left his house for his pension
And he found a lost penguin en route
So he took it to Sharon, who's handy
At writing out postcards to suit

So she puts in her window a notice
Saying "if you have lost one, it's here"
And people keep asking "what penguin?"
So she shows them and they say "it's clear"

But it might be a child who has lost it
And they're sad and upset, 'cos it's true
That they must see their penguin for comfort
And they can't go to sleep till they do

    So they walk down the street the next morning
    And they see Sharon's notice and cry
    "That's my penguin, they found it, thank goodness"
    Then they claim it as theirs with a sigh

    But it wasn't a black and white penguin
    It was a biscuit, in wrapper of red
    So they took it and scoffed it with relish
    And that night they went happily to bed!

So dad found this biscuit on his path, took it into the Post Office for a joke asking Sharon what she was going to do about it and the next thing the postcard appeared saying "Have you lost a penguin? Enquire within!" This poem was also bought for a lady who works in that same famous biscuit factory to display on the staff notice board!

    I'm going to throw another light hearted poem in here, slightly out of context but since I've mentioned being hard up quite a lot it's one a lot of people will identify with and it also sold well as a stocking filler. This was written around 1990.

ROLL ON PAY DAY

I've just opened up my statement
And again I'm in the red
But I need to do some shopping
So I'll go and talk to Fred

I only use him when I'm desperate
And there's nowhere else to go
Then I promise to repay him
And with interest, don't you know

Of course it doesn't solve the problem
But when your back's against the wall
And it's another week till pay-day
And the phone bill's in the hall …
Then I turn to Fred, but he can't help
And now I've really got the blues
'Cos he's a little china piggy bank
And he's full of I.O.U.'s!

Again that one shows that my sense of humour hadn't completely deserted me in those days. I mentioned earlier that there has been a lot more laughter than tears in my life and now that you're getting to know more about my family you'll understand why – we do still cry of course but nowadays it's usually with laughter and it's the best medicine in the world. I can remember many occasions now when things seemed to be at their bleakest and we'd get together with Dean's family or my own to commiserate with each other then end up laughing till our sides were sore - that was all we needed to get us through a few more days.

Suffice to say we're all very close and we know that no matter how low we feel, even if we can't always be together, we can always pick up the phone and share our troubles and almost always have a laugh as well.

Chapter 15

It's occurred to me as I write this that interspersing my poems is probably a much better way of making people aware of them because they make a lot more sense when you know the story behind them. I know they won't appeal to everyone but I think most people will enjoy them. I'm not sure at this point whether I will have them as a separate anthology in future, I may just finish up the stock I have unless there seems to be a demand for them otherwise.

I have written a lot more poems since the original anthology was made up and I now realise that I really could write a poem on absolutely any subject, no matter how weird, because I've done it so many times already and very often in the space of just ten minutes!

I've also written personalised poems as quickly as that on several occasions but I do usually like to spend an hour or so on those – it depends on the amount of detail I get because more often than not there's so much of it I could write one the length of Tam O'Shanter. Most of them average eight to ten verses though which is just enough to fill an A4 page and then I find a nice font, centre the poem on the page and print it on buff coloured parchment paper. After that I get it laminated because it protects it as well but I'm told by most customers that they also have them framed.

I never use customer's poems for publicity purposes unless I get their permission first and there would be no point in using them in this book anyway because they would only make sense to the people involved but I think you'll agree that the next one could apply to millions of first time dad's. I have to confess this is one of my absolute favourites and I'm very proud of it:

THROUGH A FATHERS EYES

There are few things in any man's lifetime
That could equal the moment, I'm sure
When you hold your own child for the first time
It's a moment that's precious and pure

Then you feel you can move any mountain
And there's nothing on earth you won't do
To protect and provide for this person
Who is gazing back, wide-eyed, at you

Though his life now is only beginning
You can see far ahead through the years
All those moments to come that you'll cherish
Full of laughter and love and some tears

And that road may at times be confusing
But you'll be there to guide him along
To explain and to praise and encourage
All his hopes and his dreams from now on

It's an honour to be this child's father
It surpasses all things I have done
So to Fiona, my wife, I say "thank you"
And to Luke I say "welcome, my son."

That's the first time I've typed that poem since I wrote it in July 1999 and it still gives me goosebumps. Naturally I've asked the parents permission to use it and they gave it willingly, in fact I have a lovely letter from them on my wall among dozens of others saying that they were absolutely delighted with it, that it certainly pulled a few heart strings and that it's been framed and has pride of place in the house.

Like I said, it could apply to millions of dads and when I first took the order I thought I might have to get some input from Dean about how he'd felt but then I realised I only had to transfer my own feelings from when I gave birth to my three.

On a lighter note now, and going back to what I said about writing on absolutely any subject this next one is about a slug! I was sitting in the garden very early one morning having a cup of tea and a think, as I often used to do in the days when I had more time and I saw this huge black slug slithering towards me. My first instinct was to shudder and think how disgusting it was but then I thought "poor soul, it didn't ask to be a slug" - so this is for slimy, horrible creatures everywhere.

FROM A SLUG

I sat in the garden one morning
And a slug came to bid me good day
He was shiny and black and enormous
And this is what he had to say

"I know how folk feel about my kind
You think we're the scum of the earth
And you can't figure out what we're here for
'Cos we don't seem to have too much worth

It would seem we are purely destructive
Put on earth to cause damage and harm
We're slimy and slow and disgusting
And you think that we're lacking in charm

But if you could see things from our side
It's not that much fun way down here
We're prey for the birds when they're hungry
Or you kill us with poison and beer

> And it's not that we chose to be harmful
> But we do have to eat, just like you
> We can't do our shopping in Safeways
> 'Cos we'd never survive in the queue
>
> When the kids are complaining they're starving
> We just have to go searching for food
> Then we sneak in and nibble your veggies
> But we really don't mean to be rude
>
> So we get a bad press, not surprising
> But I hope when I reach the next life
> That God smiles on me and I meet up
> With the sod who's just stepped on my wife!"

So there you have it – I know slugs don't wear shoes but metaphorically speaking you could say I stepped into theirs for a moment!!

To jump back here for a moment I mentioned near the start of the book that I'll have to step away from the personalised poetry very soon and it's something I'll do with great regret I have to say but I'm confident that I'll still be able to offer the service because I know of several other people who can help.

I've become very good friends with a lot of my customers and I would hate them to think I'm no longer available so they can continue to contact the shop for orders and I will pass them on. I've recently been back in touch with the woman who's already helped me out a few times and we are so alike in so many ways it's quite uncanny and I know she will do a tremendous job.

This lady actually came down from Cumbernauld to see me just a week or so after my first newspaper article – we'd already spoken on the phone and she explained that she has been writing personalised poems for friends and family for years but only as a hobby and that she also writes her own humorous poetry – based on being a mum and grudging housewife would you believe!!

When she arrived the first thing we noticed was that she had all her poems in blue or yellow folders and inserted into individual plastic wallets – exactly the same as mine! Then when we started to read each other's work there were so many on very similar subjects that it was almost scary! We were lying out in the sun in the garden here at the shop and we just kept reading and looking at each other every now and then in disbelief.

We've kept in touch ever since so I sent her the first twenty or so pages of this book last week and again she tells me that our life stories are unbelievably similar, there was a lot of mine she didn't know but now realises is so like her own.

I think it's one of the main reasons I'm so confident this book will succeed because it will strike a chord with so many people, young and old and of either gender. It may seem at first that it's mainly a book that will appeal more to women of my age and background but I really don't think that's the case. The people who read the first short draft ranged in age from twelve to eighty, male and female and they all seemed to enjoy it for different reasons. It's just about life really - the good, the bad and the ugly – and of course the funny bits!

Chapter 16

I'm going to return to being a bit serious now because this next one is on a subject I feel very strongly about and that's the state of our environment and the mess we are making of it. This one was actually published in a huge poetry anthology many years ago after I'd entered it in a competition – it was lost among thousands of others and although I fell for the old trick of paying money to see my work in print I'm still very proud of it and it's another one with six-line verses.

UNIVERSAL GENOCIDE

Now the atmosphere's polluted
And we have to save our land
From all the poisons that we've pumped into the ozone
What with aerosols and carbons
From all our fridges, cars and cans
Not to mention all the filth dumped in the ocean.

And we're felling forests daily
Then of course there's acid rain
Which kills plants, and just to add to our distinction
Some animals, the like of which
We may never see again
Don't face survival of the fittest, just extinction

Now we didn't start these battles
They're from generations past
But we have been warned and now we have to fight them
We owe it to our children
If we want their world to last
Or there won't be any more ad infinitum.

We really do have to start paying attention to this problem now – it's all very well to sit back and let other people get on with it but if we don't all play our part there won't be anything left for our children and future generations. In the words of a famous song, it's a wonderful world, and it's up to us to stop causing any more harm to it and to try and repair the damage that's already been done.

I'm going to throw another more light hearted one in here and it's on the subject of cliché's. You'll also gather fairly quickly that I can't stand them but of course we all use them regularly, myself included, because sometimes they do suit the occasion. It's when you hear the same one's time after time that they can become irritating – so here we go:

LIFE'S A BITCH!

If life is just a great big bowl of cherries
How come I get landed with the pips?
Or if life's supposed to be like a roller coaster
Why do I get stuck in all the dips?

If there is a light at the end of every tunnel
Explain it if you will why mine's so dim?
When the top of the tree is really where I'm aiming
Why do I get left out on a limb?

While everyone else lies on a bed of roses
Why am I always ankle deep in slime?
And if every cloud really has a silver lining
Why do I get rained on all the time?

Why is the half-full bottle someone else's
When mine has got a crack in it for sure?
And if being wealthy cannot always make you happy
How come life is still a bitch when I'm so poor?

And it doesn't help that life is full of cliché's
They're condescending and banal, don't mean a thing
So if one more person tells me to count my blessings
I think I might just punch them on the chin!

That was written in the early 1990's and I was obviously feeling pretty sorry for myself on that particular day. No doubt someone had just merrily said to me "cheer up, it'll never happen" or "never mind, it could be worse," unaware that what they'd just said had irritated me so much something very definitely might happen any minute and things could get worse – for them!

This next one was written around the same time and long before Jade was of an age to think about boyfriends so I'm not sure what inspired it. I'd probably just been riled by perhaps seeing some gorgeous young male celebrity being interviewed and thinking he was a bit too fond of himself or something like that.

ANOTHER DREAM BITES THE DUST

I don't believe it, it's impossible
Oh, be still my beating heart
My Adonis has just asked me for a date
I have to dash – must wash my hair
Wax my legs – must look the part
And he said he'd come and pick me up at eight

Home at last, just caught the shops
Time to try on my new shoes
But there isn't really time for me to eat
Shower, make-up, hair to dry
Then the iron blew a fuse
Still I'm ready and I really look a treat

Well that's over and I'm glad
What an endless boring night
He just talked about himself the whole way through
He didn't notice what I wore
Picked his teeth, he looked a sight
And when the bill came, he just dashed off to the loo

So now it only goes to show you
That every idol has feet of clay
'Cos when he leaned across to bestow my goodnight kiss
Instead of flashing lights and bells
All that I could really say
Was "to think I shaved my armpits just for this!"

Actually, it occurred to me as I was typing it that Jade could have written that one herself these days! That's not to say that she doesn't appreciate good looking guys of course – we often make comments about their tight bums or cute faces – but she can spot a poser who's in love with himself from a thousand paces and she is not at all impressed by them!

Chapter 17

Having got to this stage in my story I have now printed almost all of the poems in my anthology because they've fitted in quite naturally so far.

However, there are still one or two of those to come and although I will no doubt write a good many more about my life in the future, there are still a number of poems that were written for completely different reasons. For example I've often been asked to write a topical one, especially if it's to go in with a newspaper article.

This next one appeared in The Scottish Farmer in December 1999 when you may recall that there was a lot of bad feeling about a glut of turkeys being sold in the supermarkets that had been imported from abroad.

THE FARMERS BLUES

Of all the other jobs in life, who'd be a farmer?
It's a thankless task, no matter what they do
With early morning starts in any weather
You'd have to be a nutter wouldn't you?!

The work is hard with scant reward for all the labour
Tending animals or harvesting the grain
Then the market price is not what they expected
Or the crops are really knackered by the rain!

Then of course there's good old EU legislation
And their ban on beef because of BSE
Our foreign 'friends' refusing to import it
But they send their bloody turkeys over here!

So to farmers everywhere we should say thank you
For all the crap and disappointment they endure
It's a dirty job, but someone's got to do it
And we'd be up the creek without them that's for sure!

This being a farming community you won't be surprised to hear I got some very complimentary comments about that one!

I don't pretend to understand a lot of what's going on in the world – most of it is so shocking I don't want to hear about it and if it's anything to do with politics and government it just bores me rigid. However, some of the news does filter through to me occasionally and I really do feel for our farmers, they have a hard life and they don't always get the recognition they deserve.

Having just printed that last piece about the problem's farmers have faced in the past two decades or so, I don't think they could possibly compare to the horror of what is happening now with the recent outbreak of foot and mouth disease.

There can be very few people world-wide who are not aware of the devastation this disease has caused throughout large areas of Britain and it is a subject I feel qualified to write about because our beautiful little village is sitting right in the centre of the worst affected area in Scotland.

As yet we are unaffected, the nearest outbreak being some fifteen miles away still, but it is quite terrifying to watch the news and see how it is creeping closer every day.

For weeks now the surrounding farms have had the disinfected straw and mats, some farmers have almost barricaded themselves in and are allowing very restricted movement of any traffic.

The general atmosphere is one of fear and sadness and I've even been aware of people talking in hushed tones, almost as though talking out loud about the horror will bring it closer still.

Added to this there is the knock-on effect being caused to so many other businesses such as forestry, fencing, feed suppliers, hauliers and so many others connected with the farming industry.

I can't begin to describe the feelings of despair and frustration, of having to sit back helplessly, knowing there is nothing we can do to stop it

As well as that of course there is also the horrendous situation facing our tourist industry. This has been affected to an even greater degree because the way the news is being reported it would appear that Dumfries and Galloway should be treated like a leper colony by the rest of the world.

As if we don't have enough problems at the moment these reports are leading people to believe that our beautiful countryside is completely out of bounds when in fact we are still very much open for business and would welcome tourists with open arms.

Naturally there are restrictions on farmland and forestry areas but there are still so many other things on offer here and it is heartbreaking to see our tourist industry coming to a complete standstill.

I know all the hotels, holiday lets and bed and breakfast establishments here in the village have suffered greatly in recent weeks with either very few bookings or dozens of cancellations, even my shop has been affected by the lack of passing trade.

Although I am in a slightly more fortunate position because most of my orders come over the phone or through the mail I am still feeling the pinch. By this time last year I'd had dozens of visitors but so far all I've had recently are local people, just dropping in for a chat, and of course most of the conversations these days centre around the foot and mouth outbreak.

As I said though, there is nothing we can do but sit and wait, and although things will eventually get back to normal for some of us we should always bear in mind those unfortunate people whose lives will never be the same again after this.

Speaking of my ignorance of world events though, it's not always that I'm not interested or don't care, I just rarely find the time to sit and read a paper these days although I do try to do the crossword now and then.

It's much the same with Dean but he has more chance of keeping up by listening to his car radio - what we normally do is buy a Sunday paper and leave it in the loo – it takes all week to read it but it's the only place we get peace!

I mentioned a while back that I hate shopping these days and that applies to shopping for myself as well – Dean thinks he's probably the only man in the world who's wife has to be dragged in to shops to buy things for herself! I just haven't got the patience any more so if I have to do it I literally stand in the doorway and scan the rails and if something doesn't really jump out at me I don't go in.

Occasionally I'll see something I like in the window, in which case I go straight in, buy that and leave without looking at anything else. Dean has given up now and just buys a lot of my clothes for me, he brings them home and keeps the receipts in case there's something I don't like but nine times out of ten he gets it right. I'm not a great one for dressing up much, I usually wear jeans and sweatshirts all the time because as far as I'm concerned I have no need to impress anyone so why bother?

It also has the advantage that when I do get all dolled up people actually notice because it appears I 'scrub up well'!
The fact is I honestly don't care what people think about how I look, on the inside I'm a pretty decent person which is really all that counts in the long run and this next poem was written along those lines very recently:

HOW TO BE UNIQUE

In these days where everybody follows fashion
It's important to remember who you are
Don't get brainwashed by the magazines and adverts
That tell you how to dress to be a star

If you want to be accepted, they will tell you
That you have to wear a certain style of clothes
You must be thin and so you permanently diet
Pierce your eyebrows or your navel or your nose

Then of course there is the older generation
Who are told what car to drive, what goods to buy
Their mission is to keep up with the Joneses
But do they ever stop and ask themselves just why?

Now of course we all must have our creature comforts
And it's nice to know we look good when we dress
But the person who's inside is more important
You're the only one you really should impress

What you wear and what you have just shouldn't matter
Don't be afraid to make a stand and be yourself
Trust your instincts and be glad that you are different
Be proud to know you're not the same as someone else.

So there! As you will have guessed I don't rush out to buy the latest in anything, be it clothes, make-up, cars or furnishings. Our house is in a dreadful state of chaos, we've barely got a matching set of plates in the kitchen and we don't even have two chairs that are the same but we still get by.

One day soon the whole house will be transformed and we will have a lovely new fitted kitchen with all 'mod cons', new furniture and carpets and it will be completely decorated throughout but when that day comes I will expect at least ten years service from everything!

I'm a great believer in the old saying "if it ain't broke, don't fix it" so I very definitely will not be keeping up with the Joneses or anyone else – in fact I often feel sorry for people who think material things are important because they really can let it rule their lives to such an extent that they're barely aware of the wonderful things around them that don't cost a thing.

Chapter 18

Having printed my poems about being 40 and the updated version on growing old disgracefully I thought I might just mention that I recently celebrated my 45th birthday – over a period of three days I have to say! The main event was on the actual day when I invited loads of friends to a party in the pub. My pal Julie gave me a new haircut and a makeover then I put on my 'little black number' and my dancing shoes and strutted my stuff till about 2am. After that a few of us came in here to the shop and carried on for another couple of hours, listening to a load of knackered old albums and singles and singing at the pitch of our lungs - I don't know what the neighbours thought but we certainly enjoyed ourselves. I got some great cards and presents too, one of them being my very own pool cue at last and needless to say it's been put to use a great many times already!

At the moment it's only 6am and I've sneaked along early to get on with this before the shop gets busy. I love working at this time of day, strolling down the street while it's still almost dark and hearing the birds wake up, there's barely a soul to be seen and hardly a car on the road. Then I come in here and go through the usual routine of switching on the kettle, the computer and the gas heater, putting the open sign in the window, making a cup of tea and lighting a ciggie. That last one is not to be recommended of course because it's a filthy habit and one that I really would like to give up one day but for the moment I'm still sitting here like Fagash Lil with a pen behind my ear!

Whenever I do get the chance to come in this early I can often get more work done before nine than I do all day and it's no hardship to me to get up in the mornings. I enjoy a lie in sometimes but if my brain switches on in the early hours there's no point in me tossing and turning and disturbing Dean so it makes sense for me just to get up and get on with my work. We had space for a study in our last house so I often used to be in there at all hours, sometimes when I couldn't get to sleep at night so I'd work till two or three in the morning but there isn't the room in our new house which is why I come along here.

Anyway, I've left them all snoring at home because the children are on holiday from school for a few days and Dean doesn't have to be at work too early.

The usual routine when they wake is that Rory has his breakfast – this can take him up to half an hour because he's usually mesmerised by the telly and when he gets dressed it can take just as long for the same reason.

It can be very frustrating for me some mornings when I'm all ready to go and he's still only got one sock on.

It doesn't help either that he lounges on the sofa and calls out to me every now and then, a long drawn out

"Muuu-uum," and I keep going in to see what he wants. Then it dawns on me that I shouldn't be running after him because I'm usually trying to do about four things at once in the kitchen but he did make me laugh the other morning when I gave him a lecture about it. I accused him of sitting there like Lord Muck while I was rushing around like a headless chicken and that in future he should come to me.

He looked at me with his big, sad eyes and didn't say a word so I flounced out of the room but just a moment or so later his little voice came again,

"Muu-uum"

Without thinking I called back to him sharply and said "What?"

Back came his little voice

"Who's Lord Muck?!"

He'd obviously been sitting there thinking about it and my lecture had gone right over his head but I just had to laugh. Like I said before, he's too cute to stay angry with for long.

I love the things children say in complete innocence, I could fill a few chapters with some of them that my own children have said never mind anyone else's.

Just to give one example I can remember from many years ago was when Lee overheard a conversation about someone who'd had an electric shock. One of the people talking remarked that it was just as well this person had been wearing rubber soles so after thinking about it for a while Lee came to me and asked why the man in question had been wearing Robert's old shoes!

Chapter 19

You'll have noticed I'm very fond of exclamation marks – I just can't seem to resist them when I'm writing and you wouldn't believe how many I've already deleted when I've been proof reading this!

See, there I go again.

Right, I'm going to print another poem here, not exactly in context or topical for summer but I wrote it last October when all those awful adverts started to appear on telly trying to brainwash people, especially children, about what they can have for Christmas:

GOODWILL TO ALL ADVERTISERS!

It's October and the autumn is upon us
The icy rain and winds have now arrived
You turn the heating up and close the curtains
Switch the telly on and curl up by the fire.

You think you'd like to watch a decent movie
Or some comedy to brighten up your day
But the children want to watch the cartoon channel
And in the end you let them have their way.

It's then you know the nightmare's really started
You try to close your ears but no such luck
They're advertising Christmas toys for children
With voices that would make you want to chuck!

They simper over Barbie and her boyfriend
A wally who's called Ken, I do believe
And they try to tell you Action Man is macho
But all it does is make me want to heave!

Then there's every furry thing you can imagine
Doing tricks and turning cartwheels on the spot
There's even, screaming, crying, wetting babies
We've enough of that in real life – thanks a lot

They advertise a tacky plastic robot
Or cars that have to be remote controlled
Then the children want to write their list for Santa
The thought of which just makes your blood run cold!

And you'd like to make some very firm objections
But your voice can barely rise above a squeak
Because the cost of these incredible new play things
Is enough to feed a family for a week!

So I'd like to sympathise with every parent
Whose credit cards are all about to melt
Just turn the telly off and try deep breathing
And failing that just pour yourselves a belt!!

And that's what I think about those adverts! I'm going to stop apologising for getting on my soap box because I shall no doubt keep doing it anyway but over the past decade and more I've become more and more incensed by the fact that Christmas is now so commercialised that the real meaning behind it has been completely lost and that every one of us seems to have fallen into this trap.

I sent the following piece to a woman who is the editor of a Scottish based glossy magazine called Hiya, she'd read about me in another paper and was intrigued enough to contact me to ask if she could write an article in her own publication.

The thing I really liked about her article was that I'd sent her a copy of the first draft of this book and she picked up on the fact that my work is not just about poetry but mentioned some of the other 'stuff' which has in turn intrigued a few more people.

Anyway, because I've always had a notion to write articles for magazines and newspapers I sent her this to see what she'd think. Although I did nothing further with it she suggested I should try and see what other editors thought. It more or less repeats the poem's sentiments but this was what inspired that in the first place:

I DO LOVE CHRISTMAS – HONEST! (BUT IS IT SUBLIME OR SUBLIMINAL?)

I know I'm not the only parent who objects to Christmas starting in September, there must be millions of us in Britain alone, but are we in a minority? If not then how come the shops are getting away with it year after year and isn't it about time we objected more strongly instead of allowing ourselves to be dragged along by it?

How many of us have been told smugly by someone at the end of August/September that they've done all their Christmas shopping already and they seem to think they deserve a pat on the back for it – slap on the wrist more like!

The reason most of them give is that they couldn't possibly afford to leave it all to the last minute which is understandable up to a point but as far as I'm aware it isn't a criminal offence yet if you don't 'keep up with the Joneses' on what you spend on presents.

As for TV advertising – pass me a bucket please! They show these sickly sweet children who are obviously the offspring of The Stepford Wives with voices and smiles that just make you want to chuck up and they expect us to believe that children like this really do exist. If any of my children had ever sounded remotely like one of these mini TV stars I would have insisted on having their DNA checked.

As for the type of toys – where the hell do they get these ideas from? Dolls that are supposedly so lifelike that you suspect when mummy junior gets bored with it, usually about three days after Christmas, and decides to leave it dumped on the doorstep you could well be visited by Social Services and accused of neglect. These dolls wet, burp and barf for Pete's sake – as if we don't get enough of that in real life.

At the other end of the scale we have to suspend belief altogether with the bimbo teenage dolls and their wimpy boyfriends with outfits and accessories for every possible occasion. Have you ever seen one with greasy hair, acne, puppy fat or dandruff?

Then we have robots that will follow orders and carry out your every command – but at what cost? Nowhere in the advert does it mention that they will be precious little use when you open your next credit card statement – unless they've been programmed to shove smelling salts under your nose!

The truth is we've all lost the plot.

These ridiculous stories of parents who queue for hours waiting for the latest delivery of the latest model of over priced plastic junk and then getting into a punch up when they arrive and there's still not enough to go round! If that's how the parents behave what chance have their children got?

They would tell you they're only doing it because they love their kids which would mean that those of us who are not prepared to be blackmailed or humiliated into such behaviour don't care about ours. In the words of Buzz Lightyear I love my kids "to infinity and beyond" but there hasn't been a toy invented yet that would cause me to kick seven bells out of another mum just to get it first.

We've allowed ourselves to be swept along with it for so many years now that we feel there's no going back but I'm willing to bet that many thousands of us would like to turn the clock back or at least slow it down.

The circumstances of Jesus' birth could not have been any simpler or more lowly and it's because of that story that we celebrate Christmas now – where did we go so wrong?

OK, that was the piece I wrote and guess what we bought Rory for Christmas? We got him the aforementioned robot (under protest from me I have to say) and sure enough, he lost interest in it after just a few days.

I'm telling you that to let you see that we do get swept along ourselves as well but there are times when we dig our heels in and just refuse to follow the trend whether the children, or anyone else, like it or not.

The Millennium was a pretty typical example because I got quite infuriated at all the nonsense, the hype and the money that was involved. Not that we didn't celebrate it ourselves of course because I acknowledge it was a very special occasion but I remember often thinking at the time that there was very little mention of what started it in the first place and why we were celebrating at all.

For that reason I purposely didn't decorate the shop with gaudy tinsel and such – what I did instead was to take everything out of my window and replace it with a small piece of hessian sacking, a very roughly made manger scene and hung a midnight blue sheet behind it. Jade loaned me a luminous star which I stuck right in the middle of the sheet, above the display, and this was the only poem in the window for the next two weeks:

> THIS SIMPLE SCENE WAS ALL IT TOOK
> TWO THOUSAND YEARS AGO
> A SPECIAL CHILD WAS BORN TO US
> AMID THE WINTER SNOW
>
> HIS LIFE WAS NOT AN EASY ONE
> NO COMFORT DID HE SEEK
> HIS MISSION WAS TO HELP MANKIND
> THE POOR, THE LAME, THE WEAK
>
> BUT MANY YEARS HAVE PASSED SINCE THEN
> THE MESSAGE HAS BEEN LOST
> WE SEEM TO THINK AT CHRISTMAS TIME
> WHAT MATTERS IS THE COST
>
> WE BUY THE LATEST IN THE SHOPS
> WE SPEND MORE THAN WE NEED
> ON BAUBLES, TINSEL, PLASTIC TOYS
> PERHAPS WE SHOULD TAKE HEED
>
> THE MESSAGE IS A SIMPLE ONE
> SO HEAR IT IF YOU CAN
> JUST STOP AND THINK, REACH OUT YOUR HAND
> AND HELP YOUR FELLOW MAN.

Pretty straightforward stuff don't you think? I admit to a bit of poetic license with the 'winter snow' which was pointed out by Christine because it's unlikely to have been that sort of weather in Bethlehem at the time but I'm sure you'll get my drift (pardon the pun there!)

Chapter 20

I'm sure almost everyone has, at some time in their lives, had something happen to them that makes them suddenly realise they were meant to be in that place, at that time, for this to have occurred. With me it's very often a song or piece of music and sometimes, as I mentioned earlier, it's a poem or someone else's words. I'm going back to the inspirational stuff for a moment because, having already mentioned my birthday I remember that on the Sunday night, after 'happy hour' in the pub, I went home to my family and the whole weekend was sealed for me because of one song.

I was sitting in the kitchen with Dean as he finished preparing the Sunday dinner and we were listening to a local radio station that has a religious slot every Sunday evening. We were discussing some of the events of the weekend and laughing about them and I was thinking how nice it would be to hear my favourite hymn right then just to finish things off for me when, lo and behold, it came on the radio.

HOW GREAT THOU ART

O Lord my God, when I in awesome wonder
Consider all the works thy hands have made
I see the stars, I hear the mighty thunder
Thy power throughout the universe displayed

Then sings my soul, my saviour God, to thee
How great thou art, how great thou art
Then sings my soul, my saviour God, to thee
How great thou art, how great thou art

When through the woods and forest glades I wander
And hear the birds sing sweetly in the trees
When I look down from lofty mountain grandeur
And hear the brook, and feel the gentle breeze

Chorus

And when I think, that God his son not sparing
Sent him to die, I scarce can take it in
That on the cross, my burden gladly bearing
He bled and died, to take away my sin

Chorus

When Christ shall come, with shout of acclamation
To take me home, what joy shall fill my heart
Then I shall bow, in humble adoration
And there proclaim, My God, how great thou art

Chorus

This has been my favourite hymn for many years now, for fairly obvious reasons I should think but I recall one of the times I heard the tune played on a cornet in the middle of a busy town and I broke down and cried.

It was in the summer of 1994, when Rory was still less than a year old and it was the first time we'd had a 'proper' holiday in a very long time. We'd booked a small cottage in Whitby, North Yorkshire which we shared with Dean's mum and aunt and it was while we were strolling down to the beach one day that we saw a shabbily dressed man, standing on a street corner and playing his heart out on this instrument.

Dean's whole family are very musical, mainly because of their Salvation Army background, so we stopped to watch this man for a while. It was only when he started to play that hymn that I had to walk away because I could not control the flow of tears and I know that Dean was also swallowing quite hard as he followed me.

To this day I cannot hear that song without filling up so you can imagine how emotional I was when I heard it at the end of such a wonderful birthday weekend.

One other daft thing I remember about that weekend was that I woke up at 3am on the following morning and decided to come to work because I knew I wouldn't be able to go back to sleep and when I came out of my bedroom I met Lee on his way to bed after watching late night telly.

He insisted on coming with me and it was only when we were halfway here that we realised we'd both brought our pool cues with us though heaven knows where we thought we'd get a game at that time in the morning!

I've never yet worked out why Lee did come with me because as soon as we arrived he settled himself down on one of the sofas, crashed out for a few hours and snored fit to suck the wallpaper off! Still, it was nice to know he was there all the same and I managed to get a lot more writing done as well.

I'm going to return to the subject of Whitby because it has become our all time favourite holiday resort and since that first time we've gone back every year.

None of us can really explain what the attraction is but without fail whenever holidays are mentioned in the house all of us think of Whitby first and foremost. Jade and Lee almost always bring a friend with them and last year Rory also took a little pal for the first time.

I remember Dean once suggesting a change of scenery a few years ago and thought we'd like to go camping in France but the children were horrified! Whitby is just such a lovely, friendly place and we feel so at home there.

We all 'do our own thing' during that week and just meet up every few hours to check in with each other – more often than not Dean heads for the beach with Rory, the others come and go there throughout the day and I make a beeline for the amusement arcade to play bingo!

That may seem really bizarre to some people, especially considering I never go near a bingo hall for the rest of the year, but I just enjoy the simplicity of it, I find it very relaxing and my brain really can switch off for a while.

I should also explain that even though we go to this seaside resort every year I myself can't stand being on the beach for very long because not only do I get bored and fidgety very quickly if I sit still for too long but I also hate sand!! Daft, I know, but there it is.

Chapter 21

Although I don't drive myself I have written a couple of poems on the subject of cars and they were written in the early 1990's.

MY RUSTED FRIEND

You can tell once again that it's Sunday
The fanatics are all out in force
With their buckets and sponges and waxes
It's the car washing clan of course.

They lather and rinse and then polish
The Granada, the Rover, the Jag
And they top up the oil and the water
Then a last loving wipe with a rag.

Now I'm all for keeping things tidy
And my house is as bright as a pin
But when it comes to my car I'm neglectful
And I know they all think it's a sin.

It would just fall apart if I washed it
And there isn't much point, don't you see
As the piles on the bonnet and roof testify
There's an albatross up in our tree!

But my Beetle and I understand this
Though they all look at us with disdain
She starts every time, rubbing salt in their wounds
While they have to use jump leads again!

It's a bit tongue in cheek I know but I do think men take their cars too seriously at times. As far as I'm concerned, even though I don't drive, I still wouldn't care what the car looked like if I did, as long as it gets us from A to B.

We used to have a Beetle many years ago and it was a really faithful old car, it got us up and down from London on countless occasions and we still had it for quite a while after Jade was born. Since then we've had a variety of different makes and now that Dean has a company car I suppose it looks as though we've gone up a few grades but it wouldn't trouble me at all if it was an old banger still.

I'm only speaking for myself of course because Dean is mad on cars so I think he'd choose to have quite a fancy one if we had the money but that would be entirely his decision and I'm certainly not saying I wouldn't take a lift in it now and again!

On the subject of cars there is one other poem about them, this was when I attempted to learn to drive over ten years ago – I was actually getting on quite well with Dean giving me lessons but after a while I just lost interest. I'm not sure if I'll ever bother now because I've managed this far without a license and I hardly ever go anywhere these days but you never know – I've heard of many people who've passed their tests when they were a lot older than me.

Anyway, this one was obviously inspired at around the time that I was taking those lessons in the very early 90's.

DRIVING AMBITION

Move the seat forward, fasten your belt
Adjust all the mirrors and now
Start up the engine, give it some revs
Not so fast off the clutch, silly cow!

Let's try again, just turn the damn key
Into first gear, take it slow
Left foot up slowly, steady – that's fine
Off with the handbrake, let's go.

Second and third gear, a little more gas
Eyes on the road, not the view
Stay off the verge 'cos you're scratching the car
And keep your hands at ten to two.

Now for a hill start, this will do fine
Mirror and signal, stop here
Find biting point and take off the brake
Lurch forward, you're in the wrong gear!

Wake up in a panic, this is the day
If I fail I will probably scream
I just have to get my license today
'Cos I'm fed up of having this dream!

Well the dreams stopped a long time ago I'm happy to say and in Deans' defence he was always very patient so he never actually spoke to me like that either. In fact, he would probably be the first one to say even now that he wouldn't have dared because if he had I would no doubt have told him exactly where to park his handbrake!

So although I don't drive myself I have several friends who often give me a lift into town when I need it and I have even been known to hop on the bus on occasion which I enjoy because when the weather is fine the views are quite breathtaking around here.

The only time the bus is inconvenient is when I want to go into The Artists Café to work and I have to lug my huge briefcase in with me. It started life as a normal sized briefcase but because I have so much more paperwork to cart around these days Dean gave me a pilots case and I'm often asked what the hell is in it because it's so huge and it weighs a ton.

I have a shoulder bag that is almost as heavy too, the family jokingly call it my suitcase or my Mary Poppins bag because of the weird things I manage to produce from it sometimes – I carry that on the opposite arm to my pilots case and that way it helps me to be more balanced!

I seem to remember that the shoulder bag came into being when the children were small, it had to be big enough to carry nappies and bottles etc but even when they all grew out of that stage I continued to fill it with all sorts of rubbish.

Now it seems really strange on the occasions that I go for a special night out and only have a tiny evening bag – it feels like I've lost a limb.

I know that 90% of the stuff in my bag will never be used but I'm loath to empty it out because I just know the day I do that I will have an emergency that requires me to use the Post Office account book that hasn't seen the light of day for many years or be stranded somewhere in desperate need of a screwdriver or spanner!

Chapter 22

Having wandered right off the point there I might as well introduce a poem now that has nothing to do with anything I've mentioned so far!

This one is on the subject of being overweight, something that I used to think was a cause for concern and I admit to trying endless diets and such many years ago but I've come to the conclusion that it's really not that important after all.

I think I've been roughly the same weight for the best part of twenty years, apart from pregnancies, and although I'm not exactly sylph-like I'm quite happy with my size now. I wouldn't dream of putting myself through the tortures of exercise and dieting any more so as far as I'm concerned - this is me, take it or leave it!

THE AGONY AND THE ECSTASY

This is not good enough, I decided
These child-bearing hips must go
Along with the lump round my middle
Which is really beginning to show

It all sneaked upon me so slowly
I used to be reasonably thin
Then I noticed one day in the mirror
That I'd gained yet another chin.

And my clothes have gone up by two sizes
Which at first I had blamed on the kids
Now I'm fast running out of excuses
As my youngest is four and a bit!

> So it's off to keep fit and aerobics
> Where others like me want to slim
> And the moans and the groans of our torture
> Go echoing round the school gym.
>
> We're all sweaty and hot now, it's awful
> I'm in pain and I want to know why
> Then I see my reflection at bath time
> In the mirror again and just sigh
>
> Eight weeks have gone by and I've cracked it
> My clothes are too big, I feel great
> It was worth all the bumping and grinding
> Just to prove that it's never too late!

So there you are, I've been there, done that and now I can buy a smaller tee shirt! Actually it's not that much smaller but who cares?

That poem must have been written in early 1990 because the child who was four and a bit would have been Lee and in those days I did still think I needed to exercise to lose my 'jelly belly' but I was hopeless at sticking to a regular routine.

Dancing is a different matter altogether though – now that's something I enjoy so much that I could probably win a marathon! I love to boogie round the house with the volume up full blast or when we're playing pool I'll have a jig around the table to the jukebox because I like a lot of the stuff in the charts that the youngsters play on it.

It also amuses me that they love a lot of the music of the 70's and 80's that we are so familiar with and it's great to hear them belting out the songs of The Beatles, Cockney Rebel and Dr. Hook and then looking surprised when us 'wrinklies' join in!

Mind you, I have to say the ones who look most surprised are the youngsters who have normal parents – Jade and Lee have long since stopped hiding their faces in embarrassment at their parent's antics because they know now that we're not going to change, no matter how old we are.

Rory seems to take it all very much in his stride as well because he's never known us any other way but every once in a while I see him shake his head or raise an eyebrow in disapproving fashion and he's even been known to tell us off if we let slip with a swear word on occasion.

All in all our children are very well adjusted, secure and happy with things the way they are and I love it when they boss me around now and then because I know it's their way of showing they care and it makes me feel very protected. Jade will bring me lunch because she knows I won't bother, Lee sometimes offers to watch the shop so that I can go for a game of pool to relax or Rory will rush up to me with his arms wide open for a cuddle because he knows that's all I need at that moment. At times like these I look at my children and I know I have been blessed in triplicate.

Since I started this book I've been looking through a lot of my original files and keep coming across lots of scribbled lines and it's amazing how much of a prompt they can be to remind me of why I wrote them down in the first place. If someone else were to read them they'd make no sense at all but to me just a few words can be the inspiration for an eight verse poem! They can also jog my memory about a story I've heard or something comic that someone has said but to anyone else it would be like a foreign language.

To give you an example I've just come across one that simply says 'Rory's wart' and I've remembered that quite a few months back he developed a small wart on his hand so I took him to the doctor. He'd obviously been listening carefully to the doctor explaining to me that it was a wart but if it had been on his foot it would be called a verruca. A few days later I overheard him proudly telling someone about it and saying "it's like a bazooka – 'cept it's a wart"!

There was another one that says 'raspberries and grass' which I wrote down as soon as Rory said it and it inspired the poem about him and our conversation about God.

Having just come across one cryptic line that says 'I'm not serious so don't call me that' I then went on to find the following four verse poem that I wrote just after the shop opened because people kept referring to me as a poet or poetess and even on one occasion as a bard! I've never been comfortable with such pompous descriptions so after I wrote this one I put it in the window for a few weeks to let people know that I really don't take my work that seriously.

WHAT'S IN A NAME?

There are times when we all have our good days
Although some start off bad and get worse
Now most folk complain to their diaries
But I like to write mine in verse.

Now you might think that poetry's boring
And if that's how you feel, well that's fine
But mine makes folk laugh and feel better
When they hear about 'My Life in Rhyme'

Don't call me a 'poet' I beg you
And I cringe when I hear the word 'bard'
I write just for fun, I assure you
You could do it yourself, it's not hard

I am not a great artist, I know this
I've never thought that – wouldn't dare
I just like to write using humour
And I'm not 'arty-farty' – so there!

Like I've said several times before, even though I make money out of my work I still think of it as just good fun so not only am I not the slightest bit interested in rushing off to attend poetry festivals but I have absolutely no intention of wearing long flowing robes and open toed sandals either!

I've just come across another phrase that I wrote down just a week or two ago that simply says 'smouldering dog' but it's enough to remind me of a story my friend Janice told me from her childhood.

She'd been visiting an aunt who owned a very spoilt, pampered dog and this lady also had a standard lamp with the old fashioned style of flex that had a type of cloth covering instead of the modern day plastic now used.

There was no love lost between Janice and the aforementioned dog so while her aunt was out of the room making tea she had wound the animal up by chasing it round the room till it was in a state of high excitement. The dog disappeared behind the sofa just as the aunt appeared with the tea tray and there was a sudden bang and a yelp – the poor animal had obviously peed on the very worn flex and it staggered back into view with it's back legs, tail and bum smouldering!

Needless to say when Janice told us that particular story there were quite a few of us in here who were unable to speak for a while and another friend even got up to leave in a hurry saying that if she stayed any longer she'd start 'leaking from every orifice'!

Chapter 23

I've just come upon another poem I'd almost forgotten about because I wrote this one to go on the back of my leaflets as well as to display in my window. I took it out of the window at least a year ago and I ran out of the leaflets last summer, I haven't bothered to get them reprinted because they're very out of date now and I'd have to put so much more information in them now that they'd be about ten times the size of the originals! This one has no title but it just explains very simply and quickly what the shop is mainly about.

> The Poetry Shop is now open
> Please come in and sit for a while
> There are poems galore on all subjects
> And most of them should make you smile
>
> You won't find it shiny and modern
> It's got comfy old sofas and chairs
> Come in and relax, take it easy
> Forget all your troubles and cares
>
> There's even an ancient contraption
> For music, from days long gone by
> Some scratchy old albums and singles
> The nostalgia just might make you sigh
>
> Or there might be a special occasion
> And you'd like to buy something unique
> I can write you a personalised poem
> For someone to treasure and keep
>
> So please step inside and feel welcome
> In this curious shop full of verse
> I'm no Shelley or Keats I will grant you
> But I reckon you could read much worse!

As anyone who has ever been in the shop would probably agree that one sums my venture up very well. It does exactly the job it's supposed to do for visitors and tourists as well because they are very often intrigued enough to step in and find out more.

I've had the pleasure of meeting some really amusing and interesting people who have just been passing through but ended up staying for quite a few hours – a guy called Rab came in last summer, he'd been cycling past and spotted the shop and within a few minutes of being here he asked for paper and a pen then he sat drinking coffee and writing for about half an hour, hardly saying a word.

He finally presented me with a poem he'd written about me which had my name running down the left hand side of the page and his lines ran from it, each line starting with one of the letters of my name. It was a brilliant poem and I was really chuffed – I know there's a fancy word to describe that type of poem but I can't for the life of me remember it.

There's also a daft bloke called Bernard who moved here quite recently, he writes regular poems about me and shoves them through my door, they're usually quite comical, referring to me as a winsome wench or a rhyming 'big mama' or some other such mad description!

Someone else I got to know last summer was a man called Howard who'd read an article about me and phoned to say he'd like to meet for a chat. He drove up from Cumbria the same day and the result of his visit was that we talked for about seven hours non-stop! Again he was someone who wrote verse, more as a hobby than anything else and although a lot of his work is gentler and more romantic than mine he also had quite a few humorous ones. He's actually had his work printed on a small scale in a much more professional format than mine and he's been on a few local radio shows and in the papers too. We left it that we'd keep in touch and at some time in the future we might do a joint poetry reading, possibly in his area to start with but we haven't managed to finalise that yet, mainly because we've both been so busy since then.

There have also been times when people have been enchanted by the village within a very short time of being here, they seem to sense something about it but they can't always explain it. One really funny example of this was last summer when a guy suddenly appeared in the open shop doorway and practically shouted:

"I LOVE THIS VILLAGE!"

I couldn't help laughing and said I had to agree with him then asked how long he'd been here – his reply was:

"ABOUT TEN MINUTES!"

He'd been cycling through with some friends and they'd stopped for a break so they all came in to sit down for a while and they were really intrigued and impressed by the shop but it was also the beauty and friendliness of the village that they were so taken by.

More recently a group of four people came in and all they had was two cups of tea and one woman wanted to buy one of the second hand books that are always available. Usually people borrow them for a small donation then bring them back but this woman insisted in putting a ten pound note in the box!

On the subject of paying more than necessary there have also been quite a few times when some of my customers have insisted that I take more than the asking price for my work. My personalised poems cost £20 but I've had cheques for up to £40 sent to me, my anthology only costs £6.50 but once I was even paid £20 for it and the individual poems are just £1 each but I've had several customers paying up to £5, and all of them have told me they think I'm underselling myself!

I still find it hard to believe that people are happy to pay me for work that I just love doing so much and I'm constantly touched by some of the lovely comments I get about it. I often think about others who have to work in jobs they really hate or have to put up with bosses or colleagues they can't stand and it makes me appreciate my own job a thousand fold.

I also love the fact that I can please myself as to when I have the shop open. I do try to stick to fairly regular hours but quite often at weekends when some of the youngsters are in I leave them to watch the shop and nip down for a drink with my dad. One of the reasons for this is that sometimes he comes in and it's so busy and noisy that we can't really talk properly so it's easier for him if we go down and sit by the fire and have a blether there. Having said that it can still be a bit tricky to talk to him even there, depending on what volume his hearing aid is on or if he's wearing it at all!

Chapter 24

Well it's Easter weekend now and the weather is just fabulous, there's a real feeling of Spring in the air and, despite the foot and mouth crisis, everyone seems to be feeling a bit more cheerful.

I've always loved the changing seasons and don't envy anyone who lives abroad in countries that are almost always hot and sunny, I couldn't imagine enjoying my Christmas dinner in sweltering heat on the beach or by a pool.

I must admit that I've been a bit fed up with all the rain we've had in recent years but I think it makes me appreciate the good weather when it comes and I just love this time of year when everything is coming back to life.

It seems to affect our animals too, especially Rhubarb, because she goes mad when she's out in the garden and thunders round and round with her ears flapping and a great big grin on her face.

We've come to the conclusion that she's not only a craven coward but that her lift very definitely doesn't go to the top floor because of some of the stupid things she does. For one thing she hasn't got the brains to steer clear of Cinders and every morning without fail she bounces up to the cat to say hello and gets a hissing snarl and a smack in the eye for her trouble.

She also has a habit of gathering so much speed when she's running around in the garden that when we call her to come in she comes charging through the kitchen, skids on the vinyl flooring and crashes into the wall at the far end.

There's no doubt about it, the poor daft soul is a hopeless case and I doubt if even a frontal lobotomy would help her now!

Spring is having the opposite effect on Cinders though, she seems to be getting stroppier by the day, especially when she wants to be fed and I'm considering making her a little parachute because Dean is constantly threatening to give her flying lessons – starting from the skylight in the loft!

Sophie is so slow and shaky now, although occasionally she'll have a little burst of energy and almost breaks into a trot, but most of the time she plods around very slowly, looking so sad that I've often thought about making a sign to hang round her neck that says 'the end of the world is nigh'!

I wrote a poem about her just a couple of years ago, it's rather a sad one but it sums up just how much she means to me:

MUM'S BEST FRIEND

There's a dog that I know who is nervous
Of loud bangs and strangers and tears
She was rescued by people who loved her
And we've tried to allay all her fears

She has shown us such trust and devotion
Despite all the pain she has known
And at times we can't help feeling humble
To think of the love she has shown

She's a Great Dane, she's black and she's gorgeous
Though she's getting quite grey now with age
She's my shadow when I'm feeling tearful
Or when I'm annoyed and I rage

Her eyes are so sad and so soulful
And I wish I could read them and know
Who had harmed her and caused her such sorrow
My Sophie – who could treat her so?

But she's mine and I love her so madly
She's my pal, my companion, my friend
And my heart fills with love when I see her
How will I manage when her life's at an end?

As I was typing that one in I remembered that I have actually written a bereavement poem for someone's dog which I know a lot of people will think is rather odd but I accepted the order and treated it in the same way as any personalised order.

It was obvious that this pet had been like a child to the lady who owned him and she was very upset when she gave me the details. I have to confess she was even more distraught when I read the finished poem to her but she was absolutely delighted with it as well.

I've written in the region of 300 personalised poems now and most of them have been for very happy occasions so they are really enjoyable and easy to compose but one of the funniest things about my job is the secrecy that's involved.

As you will appreciate the poems are very often for someone living in the same house as the person who's ordering it and I have to be very careful what I say to whoever answers the phone.

If the customer answers I have to be sure it's safe for them to talk by asking various quick questions but if it's someone else I usually say I've got a wrong number and just hang up. Nine times out of ten the customer works out it was me and they wait till the coast is clear before phoning me back but I've had a few hilarious moments I can tell you.

One of my favourites was a man who wanted one for his wife for their Ruby anniversary and I lost count of the phone calls and sudden visits I got from him with more details to be added.

On one occasion when I phoned him his wife was there and he obviously got into a bit of a flap so it ended with her jokingly accusing him of having a 'fancy woman'!

The poem was eventually hand delivered by Dean in a very clandestine manner when I arranged for him to meet the customer in a car park in town where they pulled up beside each other and furtively passed over the envelope. Dean actually introduced himself as 007 on that occasion!

As you will appreciate the vast majority of my work is just good fun and mainly humorous but as I've said before the bereavement poems are the hardest.

Without going into great detail the very worst one I ever had to write was for a child and I'm sure you can imagine how distressing it was, not only for the couple who ordered it and had to give me the details, but for the whole family.

I was extremely upset when I wrote it because, being a mother myself I could just imagine the pain they were all going through and it was heartrending to have to read it to them.

However the couple were so overwhelmingly grateful that they ordered several extra copies for their family and even sent a donation for a charity of my choice. I remember clearly being very moved by that gesture – to think that even in the midst of their grief and sadness they could still think of others. It made me feel very humble and it should be a lesson to us all.

Chapter 25

Well I think I've finally reached the point in my story where I should finish this first volume.

As you will no doubt have guessed by now this is just the first of the set - who knows how many volumes there will be in the future but I will keep writing, be assured of that.

When this book has gone off to the printers I will turn my attention back to my novel for a while and then have another look at the children's book I wrote. That was written at least ten years ago and I think it will need to be tightened up quite a lot to bring it more up to date but I'm sure it can be done.

In the meantime, on the family front everyone is still well and thriving. My dear old dad is as daft as ever and still keeping us entertained. He's been reading this book page by page, literally 'hot off the press' and he's been rooting for me all the way. I can't begin to thank him enough for his love and support, and above all his pride in me. One day soon I will also be able to repay him for all the ciggies and ciders he's bought me in the past when I've been skint and fed up.

Dean is still grafting away, both at work and on the house. He's still worrying about the bills at the moment but he also has such faith in me and my work that he knows it's going to make a difference to us in the near future.

Jade is presently working as a relief carer here in the village but has now been offered a job as a nanny in Germany for a year so she will be leaving within the next few weeks. I'd also like to boast a little bit about her here because she recently decided to hold a fundraising weekend for the children's cancer charity called Moonbeams and the highlight of the weekend was when she had her head shaved!

She specifically chose to have this done because she felt it was symbolic and had always thought how hard it must be for the children to lose their hair during treatment. She managed to raise almost £500 and I can't tell you how proud we all are of her.

Lee is still at school and about to sit exams, he's hoping to get a career in the travel industry and he's talked of it for a long time now so I think he's quite serious about it. He's still a typical teenager, mad on computer games and football and still not keen on spending too long in the bathroom! Having said that though, there has been a definite improvement there so I reckon there's hope for him yet.

Rory is as cute as ever, still happy and content and enjoying school. My only complaint with him at the moment is that he seems to spend most of his free time glued to his Game Boy. However, now that the weather is getting better he is beginning to play outside a bit more and he's looking forward to yet another week in Whitby in July!

All my family and good friends are pleased and excited for me because they know how close I am to finishing this now. I have to work on my acknowledgements soon and my biggest worry is that I'll forget someone because they have all been so wonderful but I hope they'll forgive me if I do!

My darling mum will of course be watching over me still and I know she'll be proud. This book is as much for her as it is for me and it's to let her know how much I still love her and miss her and how I wish she was here with me today.

The animals are continuing to keep us entertained on a daily basis as well.

Sophie is still hanging in there, Rhubarb's brain is still not functioning and as yet we've resisted the temptation to switch the tumble drier on while Cinders is sleeping in it.

The house is in an even worse state of shambles than usual just now because we recently had a damp course treatment done in almost every room and they will all have to be decorated now but we're beginning to see the light.

As for the garden, which is about the size of a cricket pitch, at the moment it's full of junk and it's a bit of a minefield, thanks to the regularity of our dog's bowels. Apparently our steps are too steep as well but more about that in a later edition I think!

Still, now that this book is finished I must force myself to take some time off so we hope to be able to get to work outside as well soon.

All that remains is to get this proof read one last time because my good friend Peter and I are becoming word blind now but another great friend has offered to help with that as well. Sue is a very talented lady who is also going to do all the fiddly stuff to get it 'camera ready' (whatever the hell that means!) so within the next week or so it should be 'put to bed'

I heard of that great expression from a reporter who also said that when a newspaper finally goes to press you've been 'put to bed' with whoever is on the same page as you. She was pointing out the fact that I had once been put to bed with Ewan McGregor which I have to say I was rather chuffed about – I only wish I could remember the event! Mind you, in other articles I've also been put to bed with Dennis the Menace and a pasta salad so I'm not quite sure what to make of that!

Suffice to say I've had an absolute ball since I opened The Poetry Shop and writing my story down has made me feel whole again.

I made reference near the start to certain events being responsible for my metamorphosis. There was indeed a very good reason for it, something that happened that finally brought me up from the ashes, and I intend to tell you more about that in the next book.

On a final note I would like just like to say to anyone reading this who has been through any of the troubles that we have - take courage.

Have faith in God if you believe in him, but above all have faith in yourself and, to use a favourite expression of my dad's - don't let the buggers grind you down!

In the meantime I hope you've been entertained and intrigued by the story so far and many thanks for your interest.

The End

INDEX OF AUTHOR'S POEMS

Have You Heard The Latest	6
A Tribute – Lest We Forget	11
Come Into My Parlour	13
Am I Alone?	19
Being 40 (The Down Side)	22
Being 40 (The Up Side)	23
Growing Old Disgracefully	30
With Grateful Thanks	33
For My Precious Mum	39
Missing You …	48
For Rory	53
One Day In The Life	61
Bliss	63
The Menagerie	67
Philosophy Of Life	71
The Lost Penguin	81
Roll On Pay Day	83
Through A Father's Eyes	85
From A Slug	86
Universal Genocide	89
Life's A Bitch	90
Another Dream Bites The Dust	91
The Farmers Blues	93
How To Be Unique	97
Goodwill To All Advertisers	102
This Simple Scene	107
My Rusted Friend	112
Driving Ambition	114
The Agony And The Ecstasy	116
What's In A Name	119
The Poetry Shop	121
Mum's Best Friend	126